NEW ZEALAND AND THE WORLD

The Search for Security in the 20th Century

Graeme Ball

NELSON
CENGAGE Learning

Australia • Brazil • Japan • Korea • Mexico • Singapore • Spain • United Kingdom • United States

New Zealand and the World
The Search for Security in the 20th Century
1st Edition
Graeme Ball

Cover design: Brenda Cantell
Maps: Fran Whild
Reprint: Natalie Orr

Acknowledgements
Thanks to Helen Collins.

For product information and technology assistance,
in Australia call **1300 790 853**;
in New Zealand call **0800 449 725**

For permission to use material from this text or product, please email **aust.permissions@cengage.com**

National Library of New Zealand Cataloguing-in-Publication Data
Ball, Graeme.
New Zealand and the world: the search for security in the 20th century/
Graeme Ball.
(NCEA level one history series)
Includes bibliography references.

ISBN 978 0 17 019749 6

1. Security, International - History - 20th Century. 2. International relations. 3. New Zealand - Foreign relations - History - 20th Century. 4. New Zealand - Politics and government - 20th Century. I. Title. II. Series.

327.93-dc 22

Cengage Learning Australia
Level 7, 80 Dorcas Street
South Melbourne, Victoria Australia 3205

Cengage Learning New Zealand
Unit 4B Rosedale Office Park
331 Rosedale Road, Albany, North Shore 0632, NZ

For learning solutions, visit **cengage.co.nz**

Printed in Australia by Ligare Pty Limited.
3 4 5 6 7 8 9 20 19 18 17 16

CONTENTS

INTRODUCTORY NOTES

THEME COVERAGE

New Zealand's Search for Security, 1945–1985
This textbook covers New Zealand's International Relations up until 2000. In this respect, it goes beyond the confines of the prescription at the time of publishing.

ACHIEVEMENT STANDARDS – TEXT

This book has been written to mesh in with the requirements of the Achievement Standards. At the beginning of each section there is analysis of how the events discussed have contributed to the development of a New Zealand identity (AS1.6) and some of the key historical developments in each period (AS1.5). Where appropriate, text headings indicate where there are different perspectives of people in a historical setting (AS1.4).

In order to try to meet the demands of differentiated teaching, some parts of the text considered necessary only for an advanced level of understanding have been boxed and labelled 'Extension Reading'.

ACHIEVEMENT STANDARDS – SKILLS

As well as general activities, others have been written to reflect the skill requirements of most of the Achievement Standards, whether Internal or External. Some AS1.3 (interpretation of historical resources) activities are contextualised, but the skills are the same. At the end of each section there are Review Activities for AS1.4–1.6.

AS1.1/1.2 Skills

- Select relevant historical evidence
- Identify and communicate relevant key ideas, with supporting evidence.

AS1.3 Skills

- Identify historical facts, ideas, and points of view.
- Make judgements about the usefulness/reliability of evidence.
- Identify simple relationships such as cause and effect, specific and general, continuity and change.
- Distinguish fact from opinion; recognise bias and propaganda; be aware of the limitations of basing views on a single piece of evidence.

AS1.4 Skills

- Describe perspectives and related actions

Note: although the 'NZ Search for Security' option is unavailable for this AS, practice tasks are provided.

AS1.5 Skills

- Essay writing – cause(s), course, consequence(s) of an historical development.

AS1.6 Skills

- Describe experiences that have shaped a New Zealand identity.

HYPERLINKS

Words in the text that appear like this are hyperlinked to websites. To access these, students and teachers need only log onto New House's website. Once in, click onto the site for this textbook. The hyperlinked words will appear in the same order as they are in the text, with reference page numbers and a brief explanation of the link.

GLOSSARY

Words that are **bold** in the main text can be found in the Glossary on page 70.

DICTIONARY OF NEW ZEALAND BIOGRAPHY

This is a great on-line source suited to more able students. Biographies and images of many of the main figures can be found at this site.

REVIEW OF DATES

Students sometimes get confused about dates. The ones we will be talking about mostly are in the 20th century. (Quibble, if you will, over the start dates for new centuries!)

- 20th century = 1900–1999

CHAPTER ONE

NEW ZEALAND IN 1945: STILL 'FOR KING AND COUNTRY'

Achievement Standard 1.6 requires you to 'describe experiences that led to the shaping of the identity of New Zealanders.'

Pakeha in particular still felt a close relationship with Britain in 1945, and they had clearly proved this through earlier actions. In the previous thirty years, many New Zealanders – including Maori – had fought in two of Britain's wars. One of the reasons for this close relationship was that much of the Pakeha population of New Zealand had originated in Britain. A second key element was New Zealand's economic dependence on the 'Mother Country'. This had come about through a major technological development in the 1880s: refrigerated shipping. In 1882, the first shipment of frozen meat left New Zealand, bound for Britain. This marked the beginning of an explosive growth in the New Zealand economy. By the early 20th century much of New Zealand's export economy depended upon the sale of its farm produce to Britain alone. It became very important for New Zealand to be loyal to Britain so that it would continue to take New Zealand's exports. Third, New Zealand was geographically isolated and surrounded, as many saw it, by potential enemies, particularly in Asia. Up until World War Two (WWII), New Zealand relied for protection on Britain's naval power, and the development of a British defensive base at Singapore.

Although the bonds with the old British Empire remained strong after 1945, there was a change away from uncritical enthusiasm. This was due in part to the experiences in the two World Wars. Another factor was a new independence in New Zealand foreign policy. This was because of the election in 1935 of the first ever Labour government.

Frozen New Zealand meat on sale in London, around 1900.

DEVELOPMENT OF NEW ZEALAND'S FOREIGN POLICY

Foreign policy is the relationship countries have with each other. It usually includes diplomatic links (where officials from each country keep in regular touch), and issues of trade, culture and security.

New Zealand's foreign policy from the beginning of the 20th century was decided by Britain. Up until at least the 1930s, New Zealand resisted the trend of taking more responsibility for itself. In this respect, New Zealand was unlike other former British **colonies** such as Canada and Australia. With little enthusiasm, New Zealand accepted a degree of independence in 1907, when it was granted 'Dominion' status. When in 1931 the British parliament passed the Statute of Westminster, giving its former colonies the option to be fully independent, the New Zealand government refused. (It was not until 1947 before this right was at last accepted.) New Zealand was, however, an early member of the British Commonwealth. This was a voluntary association of former British colonies, created by the Statute of Westminster.

With the election of the first Labour government in 1935, a more independent line towards foreign policy was adopted. As a **left-wing** (see page 8) government, Labour believed in **collective security** through a world organisation,

SOURCE A

Kiwi: "I think I would look better without it."

the League of Nations (forerunner of the United Nations). **Collective security** was a policy whereby countries supported each other, agreeing that any aggressive act against one would be treated as a hostile act against all. The idea of collective security was to discourage aggressive actions in the first place. The League's goal was different to the sort of 'them and us' alliances that had seen the outbreak of World War One. In line with its more independent approach, the first Labour government was vocal in its condemnation of aggression in Abyssinia, Spain and Manchuria in the 1930s. For its own political reasons, Britain was doing little to stop aggressors, and it did not appreciate New Zealand's outspoken stance.

Whereas Britain was only lukewarm about the League of Nations New Zealand was strongly in favour. Prime Minister Savage even went so far as to claim in 1937 that 'New Zealand could not maintain her assurance of aid [to Britain] in time of war if Britain on her part refused to pursue a policy based strictly on the principle of the League [of Nations] and of collective security.' This was a dramatic announcement and Britain was not amused. However, when war broke out in 1939 Prime Minister Savage was quick to announce New Zealand's participation alongside Britain.

The first Labour Prime Minister, Michael Joseph Savage.

During WWII, the war in the Pacific was ignited in December 1941 by the Japanese attack on Pearl Harbour. This was followed by the rapid fall of the main British base at Singapore in February 1942. Australia and New Zealand were faced with the real threat of a Japanese invasion. Several decisive naval battles in 1942, however, saw the Americans slowly push the Japanese back. Also in 1942, New Zealand considered it wise to establish direct diplomatic links with the United States. Labour Minister Walter Nash thus became the first New Zealand representative to the United States, and the U.S. responded by appointing its first representative to New Zealand. Later that same year, the first of a large number of U.S. troops arrived in New Zealand. This gave New Zealand a greater sense of security, as well as a taste of a more glamorous way of life. It also demonstrated clearly that America, not Britain, was the new Pacific power.

December 1941 Japanese attack on the US naval base at Pearl Harbour, Hawaii.

SOURCE B

SOURCE C

1942–1944: 100,000 American servicemen arrived in New Zealand.

ACTIVITIES

1. What is the link between the event described in the poster (Source B) and the scene shown in the photograph (Source C)?
2. Explain how the events that began with the fall of Singapore led to New Zealand's growing awareness that the United States was the new Pacific power.

ACTIVITIES

1. Explain the reasons why New Zealand maintained a close relationship with Britain up at least until World War II.

Refer to page 3

2. Draw pictorials that show what 'Foreign Policy' is. Include key words only.
3. What was it that the Statute of Westminster gave New Zealand when it was finally adopted in 1947?
4. What policy of the first Labour government prior to the outbreak of WWII brought it into conflict with Britain?

SOURCE D

> 'We had all the self-government we wanted. We could choose our fellow citizens [for parliament] and do the other things we wanted to do. We didn't see any need for the Statute of Westminster. We were doing all right without it.'
>
> – a NZ government official

Refer to Source D

5. Refer to page 3. Locate the key idea to which this quote refers. Summarise the sentence in the text that contains this key idea.
6. Why would an historian be cautious about using this quote alone to describe how New Zealanders felt about the Statute of Westminster?
7. Provide a quote of no more than eight words that is a fact.
8. What is the link between Source A and Source D?

THE DEPARTMENT OF EXTERNAL AFFAIRS AND CANBERRA PACT

WWII marked a turning point in how New Zealand viewed its place in the world. The government realised that in the post-war world, smaller countries would need to work together. This was to avoid having larger countries drag them again into their conflicts. In order to establish relations with other countries, a Department of External Affairs was set up in 1943. While this new Department attracted highly skilled university graduates, it also became something of an 'Old Boys Club'. This meant that it was not very receptive to fresh faces or new ideas. There was no involvement by Maori or women.

Once the Japanese threat had receded, a fresh concern for New Zealand and Australia arose. This was the lack of consultation by the United States and Britain as they made plans for the Pacific area after the war. Discussions between the two ANZAC partners took place and in 1944 New Zealand signed its first independent treaty with another country. This was called the Canberra Pact. In it, New Zealand and Australia agreed to work together on issues that concerned them. One was the weaponising of the Pacific, regardless of which power did it. Both Australia and New Zealand also supported **decolonisation**. This was based on a belief that Pacific Island nations should become independent of other controlling countries, such as New Zealand, Australia, Britain, America and France.

SOURCE E

> The Canberra Pact provided that 'within a framework of a general system of world security, a regional zone of defence comprising the South West and South Pacific areas shall be established and that this zone should be based on Australia and New Zealand'.

SOURCE F

Coming closer: The NZ Prime Minister, Sidney Holland (standing) and Minister of Social Security, Eric Halstead, with an Australian representative, sign a Social Security Agreement with Australia, December 1955

ACTIVITIES

1. Why did New Zealand set up a Department of External Affairs?
2. How representative of New Zealand society was its staff? Explain your answer.
3. What concerns for Australia/New Zealand did the Canberra Pact address?

Refer to Sources E and F

4. Explain how Sources E and F provide evidence of a closer relationship between New Zealand and Australia.

CHAPTER TWO

NEW ZEALAND'S SEARCH FOR SECURITY AFTER WORLD WAR TWO

In terms of AS1.5 (essay writing – cause/course/consequences of an historical development) and AS1.6 (experiences that led to the shaping of a New Zealand identity) there were a number of key developments after WWII.

OVERVIEW, 1945–2000

After WWII New Zealand's governments looked for various ways to ensure the country's security. One was to re-establish with Britain the sort of links that there had been before the war. New Zealand was thus quick to join the British Commonwealth. This gave a small country a voice on the global stage. Also, in an effort to keep Britain committed to its bases in South East Asia, New Zealand committed troops to a new Commonwealth defence force. Despite these efforts, New Zealand understood that Britain's role in South East Asia and the Pacific was diminishing. The United States was increasingly looked to for security, even if somewhat reluctantly. This had the effect of drawing New Zealand closer to the United State's world view, as well as its side in the Cold War. Another way that New Zealand looked for security was to make full use of the United Nations (UN). Through this organisation New Zealand engaged in the Korean War, its first overseas conflict since the end of WWII. Increasingly after this, New Zealand's military commitment to the UN was through peacekeeping.

Closer to home, there was an increased focus on the welfare of the people of the South Pacific. For those Pacific Islands that wanted it, New Zealand was active in assisting them to achieve independence. In a mood of greater partnership, New Zealand was also an active member of the South Pacific Commission and the Pacific Forum. Both these organisations allowed Pacific countries, including New Zealand and Australia, to meet as equals to discuss important issues. In addition, aid programmes increasingly focused on the South Pacific. However, New Zealand never actually met its stated commitments in terms of the amount of aid given.

New Zealand (along with Australia) continued to show its commitment to the South Pacific through opposition to nuclear testing. From the 1950s New Zealand's anti-nuclear policy slowly emerged. It was given impetus in the 1960s when France began testing its weapons at Mururoa Atoll in the Pacific. By 1987, New Zealand had banned visits by nuclear warships. It was also instrumental in having the South Pacific declared a nuclear-weapons free zone.

A key feature of New Zealand's foreign policy was that, up until the Vietnam War, there were no major foreign policy differences between National and Labour, the two dominant political parties. Both parties accepted that a closer relationship with the United States was desirable, and thus two defensive treaties were signed. It was through one of these that New Zealand reluctantly committed combat troops to Vietnam. This was seen by many as the down-side of being in an alliance with a great power. The Labour Party increasingly opposed New Zealand's involvement, and so too did an increasing number of protesters. While National continued to consider foreign policy in terms of working with its more powerful allies, Labour looked to a more independent and 'moral' position. This split became even more pronounced over the issues of nuclear testing and sporting contacts with apartheid South Africa.

Kiwi Hill, Korea. This was the headquarters of the NZ Field Regiment in Korea.

ACTIVITIES

Refer to Source A (page 7) and the text on this page

1. Describe briefly how the focus of New Zealand's *foreign policy* shifted, from the end of WWII to the year 2000.
2. Describe briefly the changing focus of New Zealand's *military forces*, from the end of WWII to the year 2000.
3. Describe briefly the changing *fears and concerns* that have shaped New Zealand's foreign policy, from the end of WWII to the year 2000.

SOURCE A

Foreign Policy Focus
British and Commonwealth
1940s
United States
1960s
South Pacific and UN
2000
Military Focus
S.E. Asia
1940s
1950s
1970s
UN
2000
1950s
1960s
UN
1980s
2000
Main Fears and Concerns
Lisala Halapua

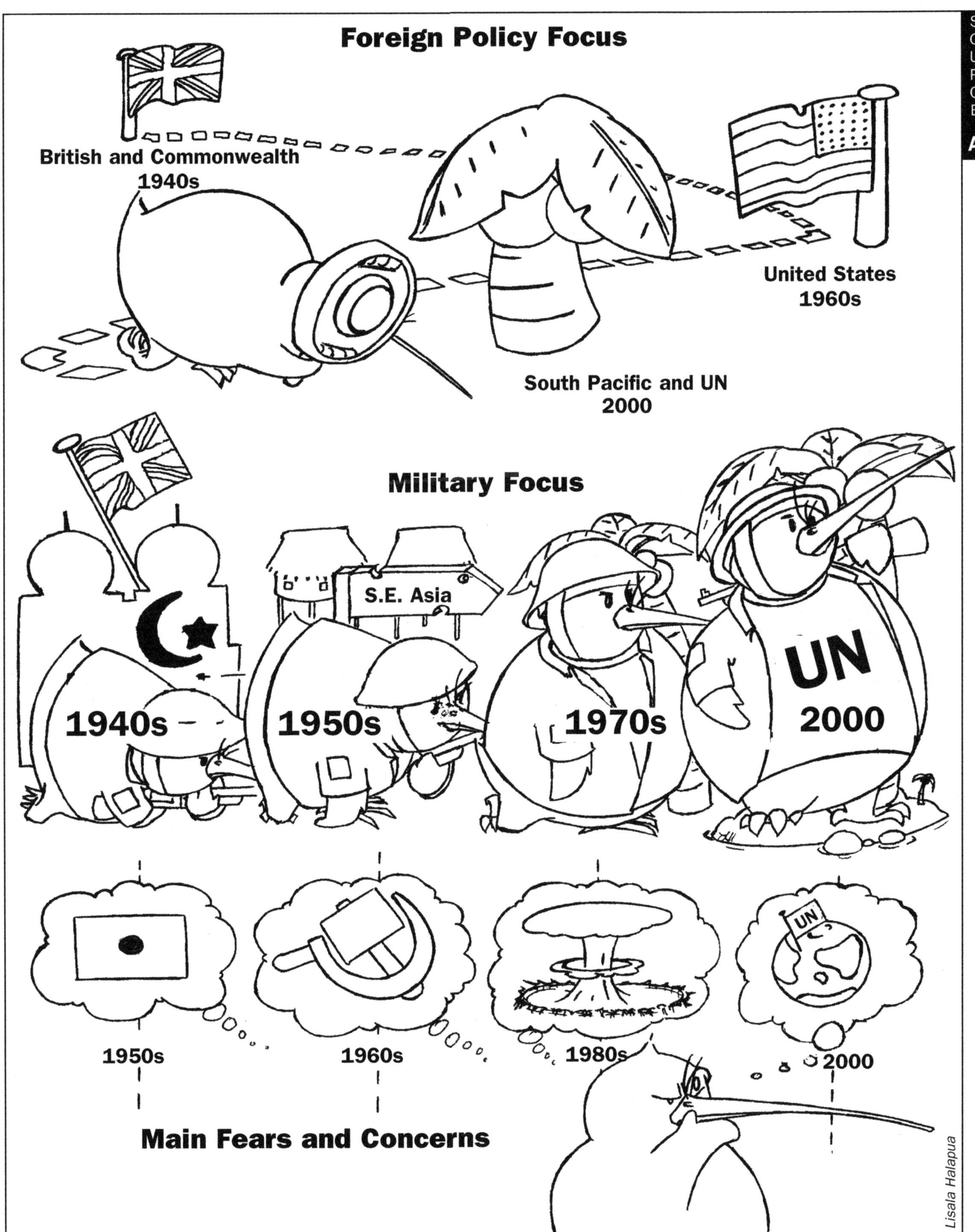

EXTENSION READING

The Cold War

Most New Zealanders became aware after WWII that there was growing tension between two very different world orders. The first was represented by the United States, which called itself the champion of the 'free world'. The countries that rallied – with varying degrees of willingness – to America's side were often referred to collectively as 'the West'. The economic and political philosophy of the West was (and still is) capitalism. The other major world order was represented by the Soviet Union (USSR) and, from 1949, China. The Soviet Union's economic and political policy was communism. After WWII, the Soviet Union had extended its control over much of Eastern Europe. The place where the two increasingly hostile systems met was across a divided Germany. West Germany was capitalist and East Germany communist.

Both sides began to compete for dominance militarily, and for influence elsewhere in the world. The resulting power struggle became known as the 'Cold War'. This was a dangerous time. Although no all-out 'Hot War' ever broke out directly between the two powers, each side had soon developed weapons that could destroy much of the world. A crisis over Cuba in 1962 came very close to escalating into all-out nuclear war. New Zealand, like many other countries, found itself taking sides in the Cold War. The 'Cold War' ended in 1989 with the collapse of communism in USSR and Eastern Europe.

Capitalism versus Communism

Both capitalism and communism are economic systems that determine how countries as a whole are run.

- Capitalism is about freedom of choice for individuals. Under capitalism everyone (in theory) has the chance to do what they want, such as making a lot of money. Capitalist countries are often democracies, where people also have the freedom to choose their government through elections.
- Communism as an idea was developed in the 19th century as a response to the huge inequalities that appeared under capitalism – the rich had got richer and the poor poorer. Those who support communism argue that there is not really any 'freedom of choice' for the poor. Communism puts the needs of society as a whole above those of the individual. The government thus decides what types of goods should be produced; this is called a 'command economy'. In theory at least, it also distributes the wealth evenly amongst all people. (In practice, communism in the Soviet Union was often oppressive.) Those who sympathise more or less with the aims of communism are often called **left-wing**.

President Kennedy looking over the Berlin Wall during the Cold War, 1963.

The Cold War comes to the ports of New Zealand: the 1951 Waterfront Dispute

The waterside workers were part of a powerful union group in New Zealand. Their job on the docks – loading and unloading ships – was vital to maintaining the country's trade with the outside world. Their demands for better pay and conditions had grown after the end of WWII. These (excessive) demands were portrayed by the National government as part of a communist plot to cripple the country's lifeline – its ability to import and export goods by sea. This was a powerful propaganda tool. New Zealanders were at that time overseas fighting in Korea in a war against communist aggression (see page 15).

The government finally moved in February 1951 to force a showdown. To beat the watersiders, Prime Minister Sid Holland introduced emergency measures that had not been used even during WWII. Freedom of speech was removed, meaning that no one was allowed to publish or broadcast the union's side of the story. The right of trial by jury was abolished, limiting the ability to gain protection through fair and open trial. Parliament was suspended, which meant that the government could not be challenged by the normal political process. In all, these measures gave the government almost complete power over the waterside workers. Nonetheless, the dispute dragged on for 151 days. It finally ended in July 1951 when the unions gave in. For many New Zealanders the watersiders had got what they deserved. Their continual demands and disruptions – and their supposed links to communism – were seen as dangerous. Others saw in the government's actions the dark face of the same totalitarianism that they had fought against in WWII.

Totalitarianism
A political system where the leader has total control. In Nazi Germany this was Adolf Hitler.

ACTIVITIES

1 Refer to the Overview on page 6. Match the first half of the key idea from Column A with its correct pair from Column B. The key ideas in Column A are in the order that they appear in the text. Use the paired ideas to write a brief summary.

Column A	Column B
Re-establish links with Britain	First major split in foreign policy between National and Labour.
United Nations	Defence treaties.
South Pacific nations	Issues of nuclear testing, and sporting contacts with apartheid South Africa.
Nuclear issues	South Pacific testing, and ship visits.
United States of America	NZ joins the British Commonwealth and commits troops to a new Commonwealth defence force.
Vietnam War	Independence, discussion of important issues, and aid.
Labour and National split again	Military and peacekeeping commitments.

2 Which of these issues do you think would have the most significant impact on the shaping of New Zealand identity? Explain your answer.

Extension Activities

3 Use pictorials and/or diagrams to show the main features of the communist and the capitalist systems.

4 Explain what is meant by the term 'Cold War'.

5 Write a 100–150 word speech to be delivered by Prime Minister Holland explaining why he needs to take such drastic action against the waterside workers. Include references to the 'communist threat'.

6 Write a 100–150 word article for a pamphlet or produce a poster to be published on a secret printing press by the waterside workers. Explain why the government's actions are anti-democratic.

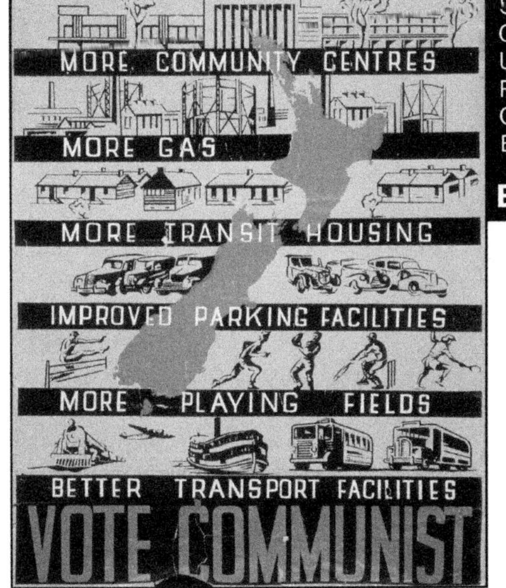

Refer to Source B

7 What organisation produced this election poster?

8 What, in general, are the sort of benefits this poster promises?

9 Refer to the explanation of communism in the text on page 8. Explain how the poster links to the key ideas about communism.

Refer to Source C

10 To what event in international politics is this cartoon referring?

11 Describe the living conditions in the neighbourhood shown.

Extension Activity

12 Refer to the explanation of communism in the text above. What criticism of the capitalist system does this cartoon support? Explain why the sort of promises made in the election poster (Source B) might appeal to the people in Source C.

Thomas Scott, 1989

CHAPTER THREE

WAR AND PEACE: THE COMMONWEALTH AND UNITED NATIONS

OVERVIEW

After WWII New Zealand's foreign policy remained committed to collective security through involvement in the United Nations. However, this commitment also saw New Zealand drawn into an Asian conflict, the Korean War. Alongside this, New Zealand also looked to re-establish the familiar situation that had existed before the war. This meant close ties with Britain (through the British Commonwealth), and support of British power in the Pacific and South East Asia. However, Britain's decline as a world power made the return of pre-war conditions increasingly unlikely. In an attempt to keep Britain from withdrawing entirely from the region, New Zealand became involved in Commonwealth conflicts in Malaya. In a new direction, an increasingly close relationship with the new power in the region – the United States – saw New Zealand sign its first treaty without Britain (ANZUS). A second treaty with the United States (SEATO) saw New Zealand pulled into war again in South East Asia (Vietnam). Running alongside these foreign policy concerns was also a growing interest in South Pacific issues.

NEW ZEALAND AND THE COMMONWEALTH

New Zealand had close links with Britain for much of the 20th century. This included immigration, cultural and trade ties, as well as shared war experiences. For this reason, New Zealand chose to be part of the Commonwealth. Membership was seen as a way of maintaining a close trading relationship with Britain. It also gave a small country a means of having a voice in world affairs. In addition, it provided a forum in which New Zealand could establish contacts with other member nations. New Zealand also continued to show its loyalty to Britain by supporting it through Commonwealth military action.

In 1947, the Commonwealth consisted of only seven nations – Britain, Australia, New Zealand, Canada, South Africa, Pakistan and India. Pakistan and India were the only member nations governed by non-whites (they had in fact become independent of British rule that year). By the end of the century the Commonwealth extended from Africa to Asia, and from the Pacific to the Caribbean. It included 54 member nations and contained 1.7 billion people, 30% of the world's population.

In 1971, the principles of the Commonwealth were set out in the 'Singapore Declaration'. These included efforts to end poverty, **colonialism** and discrimination while fostering greater international co-operation. In 1991, the principles were reaffirmed and updated to take into account the end of the Cold War. The 'Harare Declaration' also allowed for firmer action to be taken against member states that breached Commonwealth principles. Four years later, at a meeting in New Zealand, a Commonwealth Action Programme was formulated. This put in place penalties for Commonwealth nations that disobeyed the rules. Suspension from the Commonwealth was the most severe punishment. In 2000, New Zealand's former Minister of Foreign Affairs, Don McKinnon, took up the elected position of Commonwealth Secretary-General.

The most well known activities of the Commonwealth included the four-yearly Commonwealth Games and the biennial (two-yearly) Heads of Government meeting. The Games were successfully held in Christchurch in 1974 and Auckland in 1990. The Heads of Government meeting in 1960 raised the issue of New Zealand's sporting links with South Africa. In the early 1970s New Zealand's Prime Minister Norman Kirk raised the issue of French nuclear testing in the Pacific. The 1977 meeting produced the Gleneagles Agreement condemning South Africa's policy of apartheid. (Both issues are covered later in this book.) In the 1990s, the Commonwealth expressed grave concerns about undemocratic activities in Fiji, Nigeria, Pakistan and Zimbabwe.

ACTIVITIES

1 Draw a star diagram showing SIX reasons why New Zealand decided to join the Commonwealth.

2 Draw pictorials to represent the Commonwealth in 1947 and in 2000.

3 Find evidence in the text (a fact, statistic or quote) that supports each of the following key ideas.

- a The Commonwealth had grown into a large, global organisation by the year 2000.
- b The Commonwealth's main goal was to improve conditions for all people.
- c The Commonwealth's members did not always abide by the organisation's own rules.
- d The Commonwealth Heads of Government meetings provided an opportunity to deal with international problems that affected the members.

Britain, New Zealand Still Loves You! – The 1953–1954 Royal Tour

One of the clearest indications of how most New Zealanders felt about Britain was the 1953-54 Royal Tour by Queen Elizabeth II. This was a major event for several reasons. Pakeha New Zealanders – and many Maori – still identified closely with Britain and the Commonwealth. Less than ten years earlier New Zealanders were dying as part of Britain's effort to defeat Nazi Germany. During the war, the New Zealand government had even chosen to leave its troops in North Africa to fight Britain's war when Japan was invading Asia and the Pacific. (Australia, on the other hand, brought its troops back to fight Japan in the Pacific.) Also, about 75% of New Zealand's import and export trade was with Britain. Furthermore, over 65% of the country's immigrants at the time were British. Finally, New Zealand in the 1950s was booming. Wartime restrictions were over, and Edmund Hillary conquered Mt Everest in May 1953. The Royal Tour – the first by a reigning monarch – seemed to cap off a perfect year. Pakeha dissent with regard to the Tour was thus almost non-existent.

The Queen and her husband toured through 46 towns and attended 110 different functions in five weeks. In some places sheep were dyed red, white and blue in displays of patriotism. Elsewhere, instructions were given on how to plant flower gardens in similar patriotic colours. Towns tried to outdo each other in the size and spectacle of their greeting. Children formed an important part of most receptions. This was in order to reinforce in a new generation the traditional ties with Britain. It was also to show off the healthy vibrancy of the country.

All was not entirely well on the tour. The Queen had been in the country less than two days when the Tangiwai rail disaster occurred, in which 151 people died. More problems arose when the government announced that there would be only one Maori reception for the Queen. The Minister of Maori Affairs, E.B. Corbett, showed insensitivity to the Maori desire to demonstrate their loyalty along tribal lines. 'So far as the Queen herself is concerned, they will just be the Maori people. She will not be concerned to know from what tribes they have come.' Initially there were no plans to attend a welcome at Turangawaewae, the base of the Maori King Movement. In the end, the government gave in and scheduled a three-minute visit. The Queen, impressed by the preparations and reception, ended up staying a total of 17 minutes.

ACTIVITIES

1. Summarise the reasons why the 1953–54 Royal Tour was so important for New Zealanders.
2. Use the information in the first two paragraphs to devise one or more of the following:
    - a placard welcoming the Royal couple to your area
    - a poem expressing your patriotism
    - an action similar to dyeing sheep, or planting a garden, in red, white and blue colours.
3. Explain why you think it was seen as particularly important for children to be involved in the celebrations.
4. Why would many Maori have found E.B. Corbett's remark insensitive?

NEW ZEALAND AND THE UNITED NATIONS

After WWII, the Labour government increased its commitment to collective security by actively supporting the formation of the United Nations (UN). The principles of the UN were set out in 1945 in its founding document, the UN Charter. Important amongst these principles was the solving of disputes between nations without the use of war. Another was to improve economic and social conditions for all peoples. The UN policy of **decolonisation** was promoted strongly by New Zealand's Prime Minster, Peter Fraser. At the end of 1945 there were only 51 UN member nations, but by 2000 there were some 190 members. Most of the new members came from the Africa/Asia regions, as a result of decolonisation.

An increasingly familiar figure on the international stage, Prime Minister Fraser (left) shakes hands with Secretary of State, Cordell Hull, in Washington DC.

Prime Minister Fraser devoted much of his energy in the early post-war years to helping build an effective UN structure. He believed that an international organisation should give all nations a chance to be heard, instead of larger nations always dominating world policy. New Zealand thus took a leadership role in representing the interests of smaller nations. Fraser's efforts earned him the praise of British wartime Prime Minister Winston Churchill. However, critics in New Zealand were not used to the sight of their Prime Minister being so assertive amongst world leaders. Nor did they appreciate what a valuable contribution he was making. Some thought that he should spend more time focusing on issues at home. Most New Zealanders, however, supported New Zealand's involvement. This wasn't so much to do with a new sense of being part of the international community; it was more to do with the fact that the UN was similar in its aims and functions to the more familiar Commonwealth.

STRUCTURE OF THE UNITED NATIONS

Fraser's view of how a fair and effective UN would be structured was not shared by all nations. As the major power, the focus of the United States was mostly on military security. Fraser argued (unsuccessfully) for a greater focus on social and economic issues. He was disappointed in another area too. The major powers were unwilling to let a world body make decisions that they might not agree with. The most significant debate on the structure of the UN, and thus its power, was to do with the role of the Security Council.

In the post-war period the Security Council was the most important UN body. It had 'primary responsibility for the maintenance of international peace and security.' Five powerful countries sat as permanent members (Britain, France, the United States, China and the Soviet Union). Ten other member states were elected to the Security Council for two-year terms on a rotating basis. Despite the efforts of politicians like Fraser, the five major powers demanded – and got – the right of **veto**. This meant that any one of the five could oppose a planned UN action and thus stop it. With the growing Cold War, one side or the other would frequently block actions that it felt affected its own interests. This in turn meant that some countries became disillusioned with the UN's seeming inability to function effectively. New Zealand, with National's Sid Holland as Prime Minister from 1949, was one of them.

United Nations Security Council 1951. The U.S. delegate claims the Soviet Union is supplying weapons, like the sub-machine gun he is holding, to North Korea.

STRUCTURE OF THE UNITED NATIONS

- **General Assembly** – meets annually in New York for three months
- **International Court of Justice** (the World Court) – five judges consider cases brought by member nations. NZ took its case against French nuclear testing in the Pacific to the World Court in 1973 (see page 54)
- **Trusteeship Council** – took over the responsibilities of the post-WWI Mandate system. The aim was to assist nations to become independent.
- **Security Council** – the main body that makes the urgent decisions. It is concerned mainly with maintaining international security and peace.

- **Economic and Social Council** – assists poorer countries through aid and other programmes.
- **Secretariat** – the 9000 officials who make the UN run.

A related issue that Prime Minister Fraser had argued for was a commitment by the major powers to respond to aggression anywhere in the world. If such a guarantee was given, he pointed out, aggressors would be too afraid to act. The major powers, however, rejected this. They said that because they would end up providing most of the fighting forces, they did not want to risk being dragged into everybody else's wars. This was also the argument used by the five permanent members of the Security Council to support their right of veto.

Despite Fraser's disappointment at losing out on the issues above, New Zealand was an active UN participant. Support was given to the UN Trusteeship plan and various aid programmes. New Zealander Leslie Munroe was elected President of the UN General Assembly, and served 1957–58. From 1993–95 New Zealand was one of the elected nations on the Security Council. Troops were committed to UN peacekeeping actions in the Middle East, Africa and Asia. In the 1990s, peacekeepers were also stationed in the Balkans and East Timor. However, the major UN military action in which New Zealand was involved was the Korean War (1950 to 1953).

ACTIVITY

1 Create a pictorial representation of the structure of the United Nations.

- Place the General Assembly in the centre.
- Be sure to show in some way where the real power lay in the early years (refer to the text).
- Use only a few key words (your pictorial should give most of the information).

Refer to Source A

2 What does the cartoon suggest the two aggressive people will have to deal with if they attack the man standing by the wall?

3 What term from the text describes the coming together of several nations for security purposes?

SOURCE A

The text below is part of the 1945 draft of the United Nations Charter, the rules by which the UN would be governed. The sections that have been ~~crossed out~~ are the changes that the New Zealand government (unsuccessfully) wished to have made to the draft.

CHAPTER V. – THE GENERAL ASSEMBLY
B. Functions and Powers

The General Assembly shall have the right to consider any matter within the sphere of international relations.
1. *In particular* the General Assembly should have the right to consider the general principles of co-operation in the maintenance of international peace and security including the principles governing disarmament and the regulation of armaments.... Any such questions on which action is necessary should be referred to the Security Council by the General Assembly either before or after discussion. ~~The General Assembly should not on its own initiative make recommendations on any matter relating to the maintenance of international peace and security which is being dealt with by the Security Council.~~

2. The General Assembly should be empowered to admit new members to the Organization ~~upon the recommendation of the Security Council~~.

ACTIVITIES

1 Find evidence in the main text to support the key idea that the aims of the Commonwealth and the United Nations were similar. (You will need to look back at the previous section on the Commonwealth.)

2 Describe the two views of New Zealanders on the efforts of Prime Minister Peter Fraser (page 12).

3 Provide a quote from the text that supports the key idea that the Security Council was where real power lay in the United Nations.

4 What was the power of veto? Explain how it could affect the ability of the UN to take decisive action.

5 **Refer to Source B**

- **a** In your own words, what was the job of the General Assembly of the United Nations?
- **b** According to this draft (including the crossed-out parts), what organisation in the UN was responsible for deciding on any action the UN would take?
- **c** In your own words, what was the intended effect of New Zealand's proposed changes to the UN Charter (the deletions)?
- **d** Draw a diagram that shows the difference between what the draft of the Charter states, and what New Zealand wanted, in terms of power in the UN.

6 **Refer to Sources C and D (pages 14–15)**

- **a** What is the 'Arms Industry'? How has the cartoonist represented it (Source D)?
- **b** What do the graphs on the charts attached to the end of the bed represent? What effect has this had on the Arms Industry (Source D)?
- **c** How does the evidence in Source C contradict the cartoonist's view in Source D?

Extension Activity

7 Give your view on the following issues:

- **a** Conflict is a human condition and will always occur.
- **b** If the United Nations was properly funded and supported, it could end major conflicts.

SOURCE C

Between 1945 and 2000 there were 250 major wars. By the end of the 20th century, an estimated average of 500 people, mostly civilians, were being killed each day through armed conflict. About $2billion a day was being spent world-wide on weaponry. (The last time there was no major conflict was 1816.)
NZ Herald, 21/9/02

SOURCE D

THE KOREAN WAR, 1950–53: NEW ZEALAND, THE UN AND SOUTH EAST ASIA

One of the ways in which New Zealand became more involved in South East Asia in the 1950s was by sending troops to fight as part of the United Nations forces in Korea. Immediately after WWII, Korea had been divided into a communist north and non-communist south. The dividing line was the 38th parallel (latitude 38° north). This was supposed to be a temporary measure while negotiations were undertaken to reunify the nation. These negotiations failed to produce a solution. On June 25th 1950 North Korean troops, backed by the Soviet Union, invaded South Korea. In response, the UN Security Council passed a resolution calling on North Korea to withdraw its troops. UN member nations were also asked to prepare military forces to intervene. (The Soviet Union was absent for the crucial vote, and thus could not use its right of veto.) Eventually sixteen nations contributed, mostly the allies of the United States. Once Britain had indicated that it would be involved, New Zealand and Australia were quick to respond.

There were several reasons why New Zealand responded so promptly. The first was a commitment to the United Nations' notion of collective security. This had been especially true for Fraser's Labour government. The new National government, under Sid Holland, was not quite so enthusiastic. Holland's motive for participating in the UN action was more political. He wanted to put pressure on the United States to sign a separate defence treaty with New Zealand (see ANZUS below). By supporting the United States in Korea, Holland believed that the U.S. would in turn feel obliged to support New Zealand. A third reason, perhaps the most important, was that Britain had asked

Korean refugees.

British commandos prepare to blow up railway tracks in Korea.

In winter, conditions in Korea were bitterly cold.

Prisoner of war exchange post between North and South Korea.

New Zealand to contribute. On this basis, two frigates (naval vessels) were rapidly dispatched. Overall, half of New Zealand's naval force was involved in the Korean War. Ground troops were also promised. Eventually, these troops fought as part of the Commonwealth Brigade in a unit called 'K-Force'.

New Zealand's *promise* of support certainly came quickly, but putting this into practice took somewhat longer. Part of the reason was that Prime Minister Holland changed his mind several times about sending in ground troops. He delayed every time there was news of UN victories, hoping that it would mean the war was coming to an end. Holland was also concerned that the tough position of the United States could see the war widen to include an attack on China itself. Along with Britain, he urged the U.S. not to use nuclear weapons against China, as was being considered. A widening of the war would be, in Holland's words, 'costly, futile and pointless'.

Another reason for delay was because it was decided to keep the regular army available to aid Britain in the Middle East. This was where it was felt New Zealand could best support Britain's interests. Because of this, it was necessary to recruit and train a whole new artillery regiment for Korea. New Zealand's delays grew so lengthy that the influential *Washington Post* newspaper criticised New Zealand's lack of commitment. This served as a hurry-up for New Zealand, and troops were dispatched. By the time a ceasefire was signed in 1953, 38 of the 3794 men who served had been killed. (See this map and the course of the war.)

A crowd at Aotea Quay, Wellington, cheers as Kay-Force troops leave for Korea, December 1950.

Australian and New Zealand troops in Korea.

A gun of the 16th NZ Field Regiment opens up during night firing operations, 1952.

AFTERMATH

The Korean War showed New Zealand's commitment to the UN and collective security. As in earlier wars, New Zealand's contribution was large compared to the country's size. Only the United States and South Korea sent more men, as a proportion of their total population. Prime Minister Holland, never a strong supporter of the UN, now felt a greater respect for it. The war also brought New Zealand more directly into South East Asia, and helped persuade the United States to sign the ANZUS treaty. This made some New Zealanders uneasy about moving away from Britain and into the influence of the United States. On the other hand, the Korean War also served to maintain the traditional links with Britain – New Zealand's troops had fought as part of the Commonwealth Brigade. It also convinced many that communism was a real threat. This was especially so when China entered the war. However, many people also came to believe that war was not the answer to international problems. Nearly two million people had died, and the cease-fire agreement reached in 1953 saw both sides roughly where they had been when the war started.

United Nations War cemetary, Korea.

OTHER UN PEACEKEEPING

New Zealand's commitment to the United Nations' peacekeeping objectives was demonstrated early on. With some exceptions (the Korean War, Bosnia and East Timor), New Zealand's contributions were not usually large. In 1951, three Army officers participated in the UN Observer group in Kashmir, the disputed border area between India and Pakistan. Others served in the Middle East, Asia and Africa. (See the map below for further areas where New Zealand peacekeepers served.)

In 1992 and 1996, three contingents of 250 troops each were sent to Bosnia. This was the first time since WWII that New Zealand troops had been in Europe. Nearer to home, in 1997 New Zealand became heavily involved in negotiating and implementing a peace settlement in the bloody dispute between Bougainville and Papua New Guinea. (This was not *directly* a UN operation.)

New Zealand's largest overseas commitment of troops for a UN action since the Korean War was to East Timor. The tiny island north of Australia had been under Indonesian control since 1975. After years of international pressure, Indonesia granted the East Timorese a vote in 1999 on whether or not they wanted independence. Violence erupted as pro-Indonesian **militia** tried to terrorise the population into voting 'no'. Estimates are of 1000 killed and 250,000 fleeing as refugees, while 80% of buildings and other infrastructure was damaged or destroyed. Australia led the peacekeeping mission, in which up to half of New Zealand's Army was involved at any one time. This was another instance of the continuing ANZAC relationship. During these operations, Private Leonard Manning became the first New Zealand soldier killed in combat since the Vietnam War.

The government explained the reason for New Zealand's involvement in terms of its responsibility to the international community and the Pacific region. Despite this commitment, it rapidly became apparent that New Zealand's military capability was limited. Critics pointed out that New Zealand's reliance on Australia for military support and assistance was proof of the under-funding of defence. Some condemned the government for free-loading off its allies.

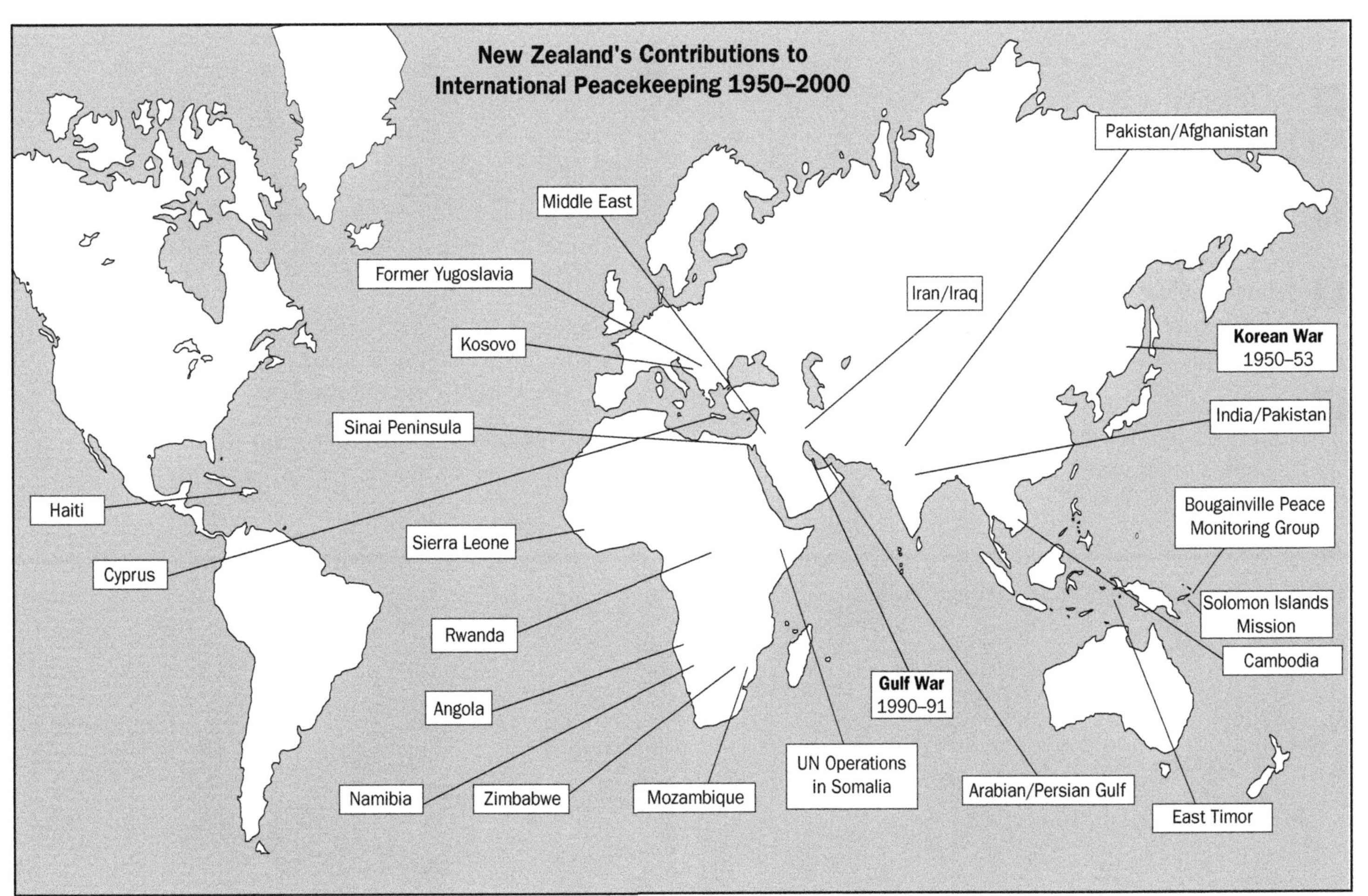

ACTIVITIES

Refer to the text on pages 15–17

Indicate whether the following statements are TRUE or FALSE. If FALSE, rewrite them correctly in your book.

The Korean War: New Zealand, the UN and South East Asia

1. New Zealand became involved in South East Asia in the 1950s through its Commonwealth links. ☐
2. On June 25th 1950 South Korean troops, backed by the Soviet Union, invaded North Korea. ☐
3. Russia vetoed the United States' original plan to send in UN troops. ☐
4. The new National government in New Zealand, under Sid Holland, did not believe in 'collective security'. ☐
5. By agreeing to send troops to Korea, NZ Prime Minister Holland wanted to pressure the United States into signing a defence treaty with New Zealand. ☐
6. NZ troops fought as part of the British Commonwealth Brigade in a unit called 'K-Force'. ☐
7. Prime Minister Holland was quick to despatch ground troops to Korea. ☐
8. Prime Minster Holland urged the United States not to expand the war into China, believing that this would be 'costly, futile and pointless'. ☐
9. The influential *Washington Post* newspaper congratulated the New Zealand government on the speed with which it committed troops to Korea. ☐
10. All New Zealanders were uneasy about moving away from Britain and into America's influence through signing the ANZUS Treaty. ☐
11. The Korean War convinced many New Zealanders that conflict was not the answer to international problems. ☐

New Zealand and UN Peacekeeping

1. New Zealand's commitments to the UN peacekeeping operations were usually not large. ☐
2. New Zealand peacekeepers served in the Middle East, America and Africa. ☐
3. Three contingents of troops were sent to Bosnia, making it the second time since World War Two that New Zealand troops had been in Europe ☐
4. New Zealand peacekeepers were able to settle a bloody dispute between Bougainville and Papua New Guinea. ☐
5. New Zealand's second largest commitment of troops to UN peacekeeping overseas since the Vietnam War was through the UN's peacekeeping mission in East Timor. ☐
6. Australia led the peacekeeping mission in East Timor, in which up to half of New Zealand's Army were involved at any one time. ☐
7. The government explained New Zealand's involvement in East Timor in terms of responsibility to the international community. ☐
8. The New Zealand military coped with the requirements of the East Timor peacekeeping mission. ☐

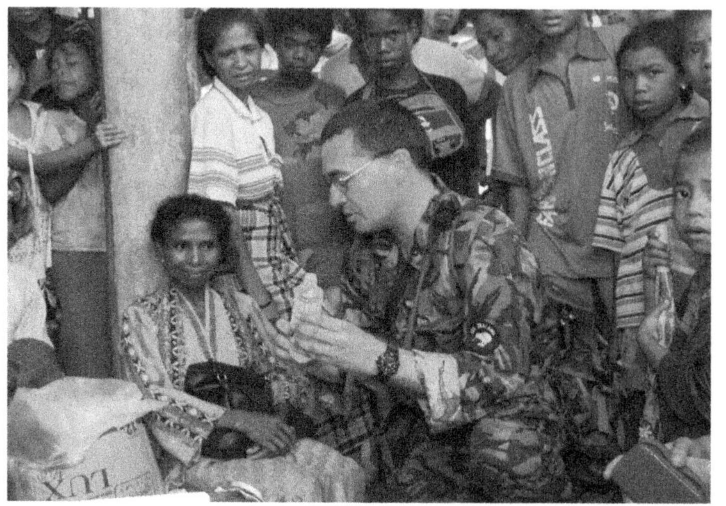

Peacekeeping in East Timor.

ACTIVITIES

Refer to Source E

1 Provide evidence from the cartoon that New Zealand's military became involved in the Gulf War.

2 What, according to the cartoon, was one of the main roles that New Zealand's military played? Provide evidence for your answer.

3 Why do you think the New Zealand deployment is so far behind the others? (You may wish to refer back to the section on New Zealand's commitment of troops to Korea.)

SOURCE E

The Gulf War

Refer to Source F

4 What country are the two soldiers from? Provide evidence to support your answer.

5 What does this cartoon suggest is the reason for Australian involvement in East Timor?

6 How useful is this source to an historian? Explain your answer.

SOURCE F

Refer to Source G

7 What evidence is there that the APCs are being offloaded from an Australian ship? (Study all aspects of this source carefully.)

8 What key idea from the text on peacekeeping (page 17) could Source G be used as evidence for?

SOURCE G

Armoured Personnel Carriers (APCs) being offloaded from *HMAS Balikpapan*. Photo: New Zealand Defence Force.

SOURCE H

Operation Farina: Corporal Fiona Thomas with an East Timorese child, in Suai.

SOURCE I

Private Mark Cramp and Lance Corporal Malcolm Smith with children at a village near Zumalal.

SOURCE J

An Iroquois helicopter flies past the Jesus statue in Suai.

ACTIVITIES

1. Refer to all of Sources E–J. Which are primary sources? Explain your answer.
2. Refer to Sources G–J. Provide any TWO pieces of evidence to support the claim that the presence of the New Zealand peacekeepers was welcomed by the East Timorese people.
3. Refer to Sources G, H and I. Provide TWO pieces of evidence from each source that show that the operation in East Timor is a military one.
4. Refer to Source G. Give one piece of evidence that shows that the New Zealand forces are prepared for casualties.
5. Refer to Sources H and I. What image do these photographs give of the military operation in East Timor?

AS1.4 REVIEW ACTIVITY

In paragraphs of 100–150 words each, describe the perspectives (views) and actions (with an accompanying explanation) for the following:

1. New Zealand's involvement with the Commonwealth
2. New Zealanders and the 1953–54 Royal Tour
3. Prime Minister Fraser and the United Nations
4. Prime Minister Holland and the UN request for troops for the Korean War
5. New Zealand and other peacekeeping activities.

CHAPTER FOUR

WAR AND PEACE: SOUTH EAST ASIA AND THE PACIFIC

> In terms of AS1.5 (essay writing – cause/course/consequences of an historical development) and AS1.6 (experiences that led to the shaping of a New Zealand identity) there were a number of key developments that saw New Zealand drawn further into South East Asia and the Pacific.

OVERVIEW

As we have seen, New Zealand's first significant involvement in South East Asia was through fighting in Korea as part of the UN forces. This was a clear sign that after WWII New Zealand faced a changed world.

Despite the Labour government's belief in collective security and the UN, National governments still sought security through treaties with larger powers such as the United States. ANZUS was the first. The second was SEATO, which came about because of the spread of the Cold War into South East Asia, and American pressure. The government was somewhat reluctant to sign up to SEATO. In return for receiving the protection of the United States, New Zealand was obliged to provide help if asked, whether it liked it or not. From the 1970s, the situation changed again as both America and Britain withdrew from South East Asia. New Zealand shifted its focus more towards the South Pacific.

After WWII, New Zealand remained committed to its involvement with the British Commonwealth. Until the mid-1950s, this meant a readiness to send troops to help with Britain's interests in the Middle East. From the mid-1950s, however, Britain began to cut costs and pull back from its expensive world-wide commitments. This alarmed New Zealand. Although the United States was now seen as an important ally in the Pacific, there was still a belief that it was right for Britain to re-establish its power there. The government felt that it could best keep Britain involved in the Asia-Pacific area by increasing its own contribution to Commonwealth forces.

ACTIVITIES

Copy or download this outline map of South East Asia. Locate and label the following places:

- China
- Vietnam
- Laos
- Cambodia
- Thailand
- Indonesia
- Borneo
- Malaysia
- Singapore
- East Timor

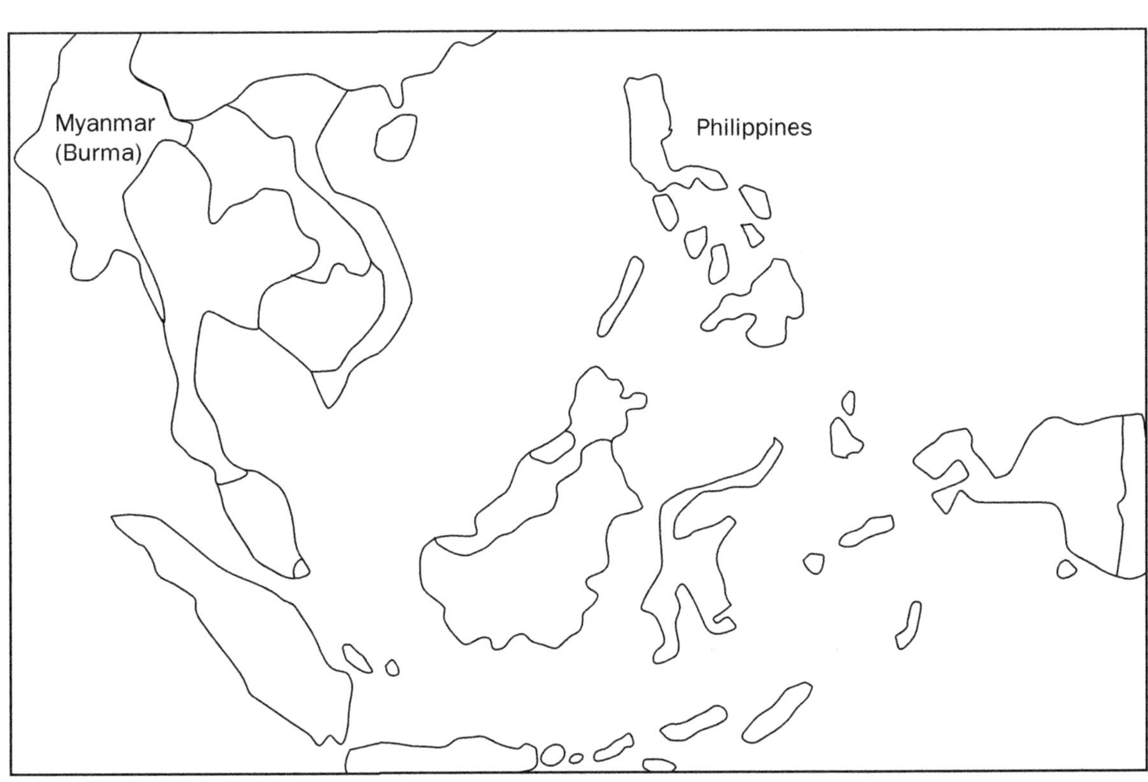

ANZAM, THE 'MALAYAN EMERGENCY' AND THE INDONESIAN 'CONFRONTATION'

In order to maintain stability in 'British areas' of South East Asia, an informal agreement was signed in 1949 between Australia, New Zealand and Malaya. ANZAM grew out of the ideas about regional security raised in the 1944 Canberra Pact. (see page 5) In 1955, it was agreed to create a rapid reaction force that could act as a 'fire brigade' in the case of any emergencies. This was called the Commonwealth Far East[1] Strategic Reserve (CSR), and it was headed by Britain. In 1957, the newly formed Malayan government asked for help in stopping the activities of communist agents during the 'Malayan Emergency'. The CSR would do this by stationing troops in 'forward defence' positions. 'Forward Defence' was a military strategy of placing troops near a potential enemy (forward), rather than waiting in a rearward position for any attack. (In accordance with this strategy, Singapore had been Britain's forward defence position in Asia up to WWII.)

While New Zealand did participate in ANZAM, the government was not overly enthusiastic. This was because of both the cost, and the dominance of Australia in the arrangement (the ANZAM headquarters were in Canberra). The New Zealand government felt that Australia's interests were not always the same as its own. However, participation was seen as both a way of keeping Britain committed to the area, and of looking after New Zealand's own interests.

The Commonwealth Strategic Reserve saw occasional action in Malaya up to 1960. Further action came from 1963 on, when New Zealand troops were engaged in the 'Confrontation' with Indonesia. The 'Confrontation' came about because Indonesia's leader, Sukarno, rejected what he saw as the re-establishment of British power in the Malayan area. He sent in his own soldiers to oppose Britain. The 'Confrontation' finally came to an end in 1966. In the ten years of intermittent fighting, over 1300 New Zealand soldiers served in Malaya. Of these, 66 were killed.

National Prime Ministers – Keith 'Jacka' Holyoake (1960–72) and Sid Holland (1949–57)

[1] The 'Far East' is the area now known as South East Asia, covering countries such as Vietnam, Cambodia, Laos, Thailand and Malaysia.

New Zealand Special Air Service (SAS) forces in Malaya, 1955.

In 1971, as the last combat troops were being withdrawn from Malaysia, ANZAM was renegotiated as the Five Power Defence Arrangement. Singapore, New Zealand, Australia, Britain and Malaysia were the signatories. The New Zealand government emphasised that the Agreement only obliged countries to consult if there was any aggression towards Singapore or Malaysia. New Zealand wanted to avoid being forced into a war it didn't support. By 1976, Britain and Australia believed that the risk of communist aggression had passed. They withdrew the last of their troops, alarming New Zealand. In an effort to persuade the United States to fill the gap left by Britain, New Zealand left its troops in Malaysia. By 1989, however, New Zealand had also withdrawn from its last base in Singapore.

> Malaysia was formed in 1963 from the former British colonies of Malaya and Singapore. (Singapore later withdrew.)

SOURCE A

> Prime Minister Sid Holland speaks to parliament after his return from a Commonwealth Prime Ministers' Meeting in 1955, which discussed the establishment of a Commonwealth Strategic Reserve.
>
> "Civilisation is today at the crossroads. We must strive to see that the seeds of communism are not sown in other countries that may bring about our downfall.... I say with great seriousness that we as a country can no longer [leave] a great deal of the burden of maintaining peace to our Mother Country.... Not only must we justify help from Britain by being prepared to pull our weight in the British boat, but also we must earn the active support of the United States by demonstrating to her that we are prepared to play our part in our own defence.... We have been invited [by Britain] to undertake a very special duty, and that is to form what you might term a cold war front in Malaya, the idea being to ensure that an enemy that wants to indulge in infiltration and subversion [rebellion] is going to be stopped before he gets here [New Zealand]."

ACTIVITIES

Refer to Source A

1 What does Prime Minister Holland believe is a serious threat to New Zealand (and the world)?

2 What does Holland mean by '[we must be] prepared to pull our weight in the British boat'? What other country does he see as being important to New Zealand's interests?

3 What significant world organisation does Holland not mention when considering security issues? How does Holland's view differ from that of Prime Minister Peter Fraser in the 1940s?

4 Reread the last sentence in Source A that talks about a 'cold war front in Malaya'. What key idea from the text in this section is Holland referring to?

Refer to Source B

5 Which of the figures in the cartoon is the 'threat' described in the last sentence of Holland's speech (Source A) likely to refer?

6 What country is shown in the cartoon as being under threat?

7 What appears to be the attitude of Prime Minister Holyoake to the threat? How does his attitude compare to Prime Minister Holland's (Source A)?

8 What feature of the foreign policies of National and Labour up to the 1960s is shown in the cartoon?

SOURCE B

Labour leader Walter Nash and National's Prime Minister Holyoake. "Better not interfere, old boy – he might lose his temper!" (1964)

Refer to Source C

9 What 'threat' do the rats represent?

10 Refer to page 22. What was the name of the military force that was created under the ANZAM Treaty?

11 What four countries are represented as part of this military force?

12 What term from the text is used to describe the positioning of New Zealand (and Australian) troops up in South East Asia?

SOURCE C

ANZUS: AUSTRALIA, NEW ZEALAND AND THE UNITED STATES (BUT NOT BRITAIN)

After WWII, New Zealand and Australia were greatly concerned that Japan would again rise up to be a major power in the Pacific. Neither country liked the generous peace settlement that the United States was looking to make with Japan. However, in the post-war world the U.S. was the main Pacific power, and its main concern was communism. It wanted Japan to be rebuilt into a strong anti-communist ally. When the Korean War broke out, New Zealand and Australia had already begun negotiating a security arrangement with the United States. The rapid promise of support by both countries to the UN forces helped convince the U.S. to enter into an agreement. Thus, on the basis of different security concerns, the ANZUS Treaty was signed in 1951 by Australia, New Zealand and the United States.

ANZUS offered New Zealand and Australia a degree of collective security with regard to Japan, and against the growing communist threat. For America, the Treaty formally extended its influence into the South Pacific. It also gave the United States the right to respond to what it saw as any communist threat to its allies. Originally, the U.S. had wanted both the Philippines and Japan to be part of the Treaty, but New Zealand in particular had protested. A defence treaty with Asian countries was too great a shift in foreign policy for New Zealand at that time.

New Zealand and Australia were looking for a solid guarantee of protection from ANZUS, but the United States would not commit itself to that extent. The Treaty merely said that each party would consult if one was threatened. This was the best that Australia and New Zealand could get. As part of the Treaty, a Council of the three signatory countries was established and met regularly thereafter. While the ANZUS Treaty acknowledged the continuing role of the United Nations in international security, it also recognised the practical limitations of UN power.

The significance of ANZUS

ANZUS marked an important shift in foreign relations, although New Zealand governments at the time did not want to see it that way. ANZUS was the first major treaty that New Zealand had signed with an 'outside' power. Prime Minister Holland was worried that ANZUS would be seen as disloyalty to Britain. Anticipating public concern, he denied that this was the case. There was also a degree of unease that New Zealand was, almost against its will, moving along a path away from Britain's interests and towards those of the United States. Nonetheless, Holland claimed that ANZUS was a positive move, as it relieved New Zealand of major concerns in the Pacific. This would, he said, actually make it easier to support Britain militarily, by freeing up troops. Despite this assurance, there was a public uproar once it was announced by the ANZUS Council that there would be no new admissions, not even Britain.

SOURCE D

ACTIVITIES

1 What term from the text describes the coming together of several nations for security purposes?

Refer to Source D

2 What threat does America appear to be most concerned about?

3 What country is shown as important to America in resisting this threat?

4 What threat do Australia and New Zealand appear to be most concerned about?

5 What country is shown as not being part of ANZUS?

SOURCE E

Refer to Source E

6 What country is represented by the figure holding the blanket? Provide evidence to support your answer.

7 To whom does the figure in the cartoon want to sell the 'new blanket'?

8 What does the 'new blanket' represent? Explain why the idea of a 'blanket' is appropriate in this cartoon.

9 The cartoonist seems to be suggesting that the figure in the cartoon came up with the idea of the 'new blanket' on his own. Refer to the text on page 24 and explain why this is not true.

Refer to Source F

10 Which section(s) of the Treaty do you think are represented by the ideas shown in the cartoon (Source E)? Explain your answer.

For each of the following, give the Article number and a short quote from the Article.

11 Which section of the Treaty states that ...

- **a** it is a collective security arrangement?
- **b** the Treaty does not require regular renewal?
- **c** there is not really any other effective means for ensuring security in the Pacific area?
- **d** if there is a threat, then each country's government would discuss amongst itself how to respond?

SOURCE F

SELECTED ARTICLES OF THE ANZUS TREATY

Introduction
"[Australia, New Zealand and the United States] ... declare publicly and formally their sense of unity, so that no potential aggressor could be under the illusion that any of them stand alone in the Pacific Area."

Article 4
"Each Party recognises that an armed attack in the Pacific Area on any of the Parties would be dangerous to its own peace and safety and declares that it would act to meet the common danger in accordance with its constitutional government processes."

Article 8
"Until ... the development by the United Nations of more effective means to maintain international peace and security, the [ANZUS] Council ... [will work to] contribute to the security of [the Pacific]."

Article 10
"This Treaty shall remain in force indefinitely. Any Party may cease to be a member of the Council ... one year after notice has been given..."

SEATO: THE UNITED STATES' ANTI-COMMUNIST ALLIANCE

This Treaty was signed after two significant Cold War events. The first of these was the Korean War (1950–53), in which the communist North attacked the non-communist South. The second was the 1954 defeat of the French in Vietnam, also by communist forces. The resulting peace settlement saw Vietnam divided 'temporarily' into a communist North and non-communist South, much as Korea had been. The United States was determined to 'contain' communism in North Vietnam. One means of doing this was to have surrounding countries sign up to an agreement that prevented communist aggression against South Vietnam. The fear was that if the South 'fell', the neighbouring countries would be the next to 'fall' to communism, like a row of dominoes. This was a process that the American Secretary of State, John Foster Dulles, called the 'domino theory'.

The South East Asian Treaty Organisation Treaty (or Manila Treaty) was signed in 1954. The United States, New Zealand, Australia, France, Pakistan, the Philippines, Thailand and Britain were the signatories. The agreement also extended protection to the countries of South East Asia – Laos, Cambodia and Vietnam. SEATO, however, was weakened from the start when India, Indonesia and Malaya declined to join. One of the aims of SEATO was to improve social and economic conditions in South East Asia. It was also a collective security agreement similar to ANZUS, where an attack on one member was seen as an attack on all. It was agreed, however, that no military action would be taken unless a threatened member asked for it. The United States also informed members that it would only become directly involved if an aggressive action looked likely to aid the spread of communism.

New Zealand and SEATO

From New Zealand's point of view, SEATO seemed to offer little protection over and above what ANZUS already provided. Nor could most New Zealanders in 1954 see any serious communist threat to New Zealand, despite the experiences of the Korean War. The government was also concerned about the cost of maintaining the alliance, and was cautious about getting dragged into a war in Asia. In addition, both New Zealand and Australia tended to place more emphasis on the social and economic goals of SEATO than the military ones. In a significant shift, it was also a treaty that for the first time included Asian countries as allies. Despite all of this, it was felt necessary for New Zealand to support the United States in SEATO, so that the US would remain committed to ANZUS. Furthermore, participation in SEATO also seemed to offer the opportunity of again working closely with Britain. As it happened, this was not to be the case. When the Vietnam War broke out, Britain declined to become involved. New Zealand, reluctantly, did.

The end of SEATO

SEATO did not survive beyond the Vietnam War. Most countries were disillusioned with the way that the conflict had gone. Britain and France had reduced their limited commitment to SEATO by 1974, and Pakistan had withdrawn entirely. America had not won the war, and by 1975 had pulled out from the South East Asian region. (Beyond South Vietnam, no further countries 'fell' to communism, proving the domino theory wrong.) New Zealand agreed with Australia that SEATO should be transformed into a social and economic organisation. This was consistent with New Zealand's view that aid and development programmes were much better at stopping communism than guns.

SEATO Conference in Manila 1966. New Zealand's Prime Minister Holyoake is 5th from left. President Lyndon Johnson is on far right.

SOURCE G

SELECTED ARTICLES OF THE MANILA TREATY

ARTICLE 3
The Parties undertake to ... cooperate with one another in the further development of economic measures, including technical assistance, designed both to promote economic progress and social well-being and to further the individual and collective efforts of governments toward these ends.

ARTICLE 4.2
If ... any of the Parties ... is threatened in any way other than by armed attack or is affected or threatened by any fact or situation which might endanger the peace of the area, the Parties shall consult immediately in order to agree on the measures which should be taken for the common defense.

ARTICLE 4.3
It is understood that no action on the territory of any State ... shall be taken except at the invitation or with the consent of the government concerned.

ARTICLE 6
This Treaty does not affect ... in any way the rights and obligations of any of the Parties under the Charter of the United Nations, or the responsibility of the United Nations for the maintenance of international peace and security.

ADDITIONAL ARTICLE
The United States of America in [joining] the present Treaty does so with the understanding that its recognition of the effect of aggression and armed attack ... apply only to communist aggression, but affirms that in the event of other aggression or armed attack it will consult....

NEW ZEALAND AND THE VIETNAM WAR

New Zealand's involvement in the Vietnam War was significant in several ways. First, New Zealand's links with the United States made it difficult not to participate, even though this participation was reluctant. New Zealand was directly drawn into the Vietnam War through SEATO, as well as indirectly through a sense of obligation in order to keep the United States committed to ANZUS. Second, the Vietnam War sparked the first major difference between National and Labour on foreign policy issues. It divided the public and brought people out onto the streets in protest for the first time since the Depression. Finally, this was also the first war that New Zealand had fought without Britain.

The United States wanted both Australia and New Zealand in Vietnam, but New Zealand's involvement was always reluctant. One of the main reasons that the U.S. wanted New Zealand's participation was so that it could more easily justify its own presence in Vietnam. If New Zealand and Australia said that they were worried about the spread of communism, the U.S. could claim that it was supporting its smaller allies. In response to this pressure, New Zealand sent medical and engineering teams. However, as no New Zealand combat troops were sent, the Americans were not satisfied. They hinted that trade and other security measures might be affected if New Zealand did not contribute more. The Holyoake government tried to argue that it was unable to provide troops for Vietnam. New Zealand's forces, he said, were fully committed to the Commonwealth Strategic Reserve in Malaya.

In 1964, the President of South Vietnam requested assistance in the growing conflict, as required under the terms of SEATO. When Australia decided to send troops,

ACTIVITIES

Refer to Source G

For each of the following questions, give the Article number and a short quote:

Which section of the Treaty states that …

1. a country that is threatened must ask for military assistance before it will be given?
2. it has goals other than just military ones?
3. the threat to a nation does not necessarily have to be a military one in order for Treaty members to act?
4. the Treaty has not taken over responsibilities that belong to other international organisations?
5. the United States is focused mainly on the communist threat?
6. governments will be encouraged to contribute to looking after the well-being of their own peoples themselves?

Refer to Source H

7. Provide evidence from the cartoon that the United States is the main power involved in SEATO.
8. What term from the text describes the coming together of several nations for security purposes?
9. What is the threat that SEATO is shown protecting South Vietnam from?
10. What term from the text describes the security policy that is represented by the water from the fire hose that surrounds North Vietnam?

SOURCE H

Background to the Vietnam War

The Vietnam War was part of the Cold War in South East Asia. The French had controlled Vietnam from the late 19th century until 1940, but Japan had invaded and taken over during World War II. After the Japanese had been defeated, the Vietnamese people thought that they would be free from foreign powers. This was not to be. Supported by Britain, the French returned. The Vietnamese, under communist leadership, used **guerrilla warfare** against the better-equipped French. By 1954 they had defeated the French. It was this defeat that prompted the United States to form SEATO in order to stop the spread of communism.

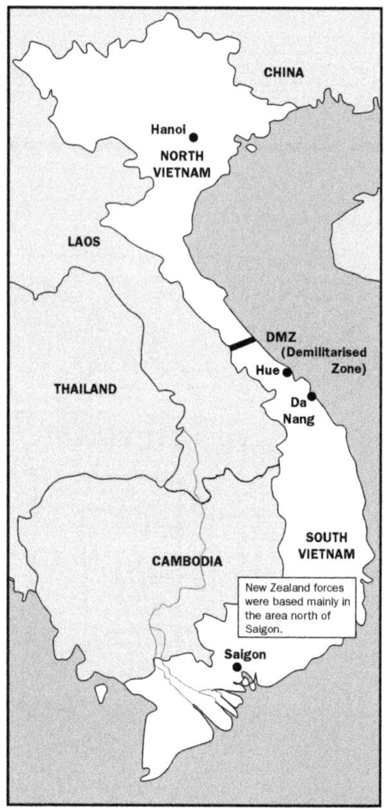

At a conference in 1954, it was agreed to divide Vietnam into a communist North and non-communist South. As with Korea a few years earlier, this was supposed to be a temporary measure until it could be decided how to reunify the nation. The war developed in the 1960s as the United States accused the North of attempting to take over the non-communist South. The U.S. sent in troops to prop up South Vietnam's government, calling on SEATO nations to contribute to the containment of communism. The U.S. was determined to prevent the 'domino theory' from becoming reality.

Ho Chi Minh: he led his people to victory despite the technological and military superiority of the American forces.

New Zealand felt that it had no choice. An artillery battery of 120 men was sent in 1965, eventually totalling 550. These troops fought under Australian command in the renamed ANZAC Infantry battalion. More pressure went on in the next two years, and additional commitments of troops were made. Two Rifle Companies, Victor and Whiskey, were sent in 1967. These soldiers were all volunteers, and all up a total of 3500 men served. Unlike Australia and the United States, New Zealand did not **conscript** its soldiers. New Zealand's troop commitment was not a large one, but it eased US grumblings. By the time the last New Zealand troops were withdrawn in December 1972, 35 had been killed (including one female nurse) and 187 wounded.

Those who did return came home to a hostile reception. They were accused of being war-mongers and 'baby-killers'. The government did not even formally welcome the soldiers home. This indicates the level of division that involvement in the war had caused. It was not until 1998 that an official welcoming ceremony was conducted. Vietnam veterans have had an ongoing battle to get compensation for war-related conditions such as Agent Orange poisoning.

The National Government's Position

Holyoake's National government had no real enthusiasm for the Vietnam War, but found itself having to publicly support it. This was especially so when Lyndon Johnson, the U.S. President, visited in 1966 to urge greater New Zealand participation. He was greeted by cheering crowds. Conservative members of the government took this as a sign of the public's willingness to stay in the war. National's victory in the 1966 election seemed to confirm this. Those in favour of New Zealand participating in the war argued that New Zealand had to play its part in the world, especially in stopping the spread of communism. They said that the North Vietnamese communists were clearly the aggressors, and it was New Zealand's duty as part of SEATO to help the United States. Publicly, this was the position the National government took.

Privately, Holyoake and other key officials wanted to limit involvement. Partly this was because they did not have a strong belief in the 'domino theory'. Nor were they entirely convinced that distant communism was a significant threat to New Zealand. In addition, the government was aware that involvement in wars was a costly business, and it felt that New Zealand could ill-afford it. This was especially so as the United States considered expanding the war into China. To the horror of many countries, including New Zealand, the U.S. again talked of using nuclear weapons. Holyoake, however, continued to defend participation in a war that he did not really agree with. His position became even more difficult when it became clear that the U.S. was not winning. Holyoake had discovered the downside of being in an alliance with a much larger power. There was the expectation that New Zealand would support its larger ally, even if it did not entirely agree with the action.

ACTIVITIES

1 Refer to the text on pages 27–28. Match the sentence starter from Column A with the correct ending from Column B. (Be careful – some are similar, but not the same!)

Column A	Column B
New Zealand's involvement in Vietnam came about because...	... America applied pressure for a contribution to the war in Vietnam.
New Zealand's involvement in Vietnam was significant politically because...	... of New Zealand's commitment to the Commonwealth Strategic Reserve in Malaya.
America wanted to contain communism because...	... of obligations under SEATO, and indirectly through a commitment to ANZUS.
America wanted both Australia and New Zealand in Vietnam because...	... it could more easily justify its own presence in Vietnam
New Zealand committed medical and engineering teams to Vietnam because...	... it saw the first major division between National and Labour on a foreign policy issue.
The Holyoake government argued that New Zealand could not send combat troops to Vietnam because ...	... the President of South Vietnam requested assistance, and Australia had made the decision to do so.
New Zealand eventually committed combat troops because...	... of a belief in the domino theory.

SOURCE I

Prime Minister Holyoake outlined in 1965 his seven main reasons for making a military commitment to Vietnam.

- **a** "...the Government must always be concerned with the security of the people of New Zealand, both short-term and *long-term*."
- **b** "... New Zealand's first line of defence is in South East Asia...."
- **c** "... the war in Vietnam is not a civil war or a popular rising.... It is a ruthless Communist aggression directed and supplied by Communist North Vietnam...."
- **d** "... the South Vietnamese are fighting for their freedom and liberty."
- **e** "... events in Vietnam affect New Zealand just as much as events in Malaysia, and indeed at this stage probably more so."
- **f** "... the New Zealand Government has a fervent [strong] wish to bring about a peaceful settlement which will guarantee the territorial integrity [borders] of South Vietnam and of the neighbouring countries in that area."
- **g** "... the independence of the people of South Vietnam must be safeguarded. It cannot be safeguarded with words. At present it can only be done with military means."

Refer to Source I

2 Which of the reason(s) given by Prime Minister Holyoake for joining the Vietnam War are most likely linked to the key ideas of:

- **a** containment.
- **b** domino theory.
- **c** forward defence.
- **d** collective security.

New Zealand medical team working in Vietnam, 1969.

The Labour Party's Position

The Labour Opposition did not feel the same sense of obligation to the United States. It argued that the war was morally wrong. Labour urged instead that a non-military solution be found, using the Commonwealth and the United Nations. However, it reluctantly supported sending the first non-combat units in 1964.

Labour's Norman Kirk, Prime Minister from 1972 until his untimely death in 1974

As the war progressed and the brutal images were played out on television (for the first time), Labour's opposition to the conflict grew. Many now saw the war as an attempt by a bullying United States to impose its views and beliefs on the Vietnamese people. Norman Kirk, the new Labour leader, called for the withdrawal of New Zealand troops. This call was joined by church groups, students and an increasing number of the public.

By the late 1960s, protest marches were being held in the main centres. They linked into the mass demonstrations taking place in America. The largest demonstration in New Zealand took place in 1971, even though New Zealand troops were already being withdrawn.

Labour became the government in 1972 and Prime Minister Kirk withdrew the remaining units. When the United States resumed its bombing campaign in North Vietnam, Labour, unlike National, was publicly critical. This was despite the risk of offending the United States. In addition, Kirk established diplomatic relations with both communist China and the Soviet Union. This was something previous governments had not done, again for fear of offending the United States. Government money was put aside to help the rebuilding of Vietnam once the war ended. Along with Australia, Kirk agreed that SEATO should become a non-military organisation to help poorer countries socially and economically. To back his opinion, he refused to host the 1974 SEATO Council in Wellington.

These were bold moves that could have angered America, but New Zealand suffered no reprisals. This was because the international situation had changed. The United States, China and Russia were now all looking to co-operate more, rather than engage in conflict.

Aftermath

The Vietnam War divided New Zealand as no other foreign policy issue had before. Although National had regularly accused Labour of being 'soft on communism', National and Labour had mostly agreed on foreign policy. In part this was because Labour had been out of power for all but three years (1957–60) between 1949 and 1972. However, there was a shared belief that 'forward defence' in Asia, collective security involving a larger ally, and a close relationship with Australia were all fundamental. Increasingly, though, Labour looked to take a *moral* position on issues, even if this meant offending traditional allies. National's view, however, was that a small country like New Zealand had to acknowledge that it depended on its bigger allies, and therefore work closely with them. National's view has been called pragmatic, meaning that it was a practical approach that acknowledged New Zealand's vulnerability.

By the end of the Vietnam War in the early 1970s, New Zealand's links with Britain had loosened considerably. For one thing, New Zealand had fought alongside the United States in the war (not Britain). At the same time, bonds with Australia had tightened through serving together in the ANZAC Infantry Battalion. The new Labour government under Norman Kirk also took a much more internationalist and moral approach to foreign affairs. This was in part because of the failure of SEATO – a *military* alliance – to solve the problems of Vietnam. It was also a realisation that Britain in the early 1970s was turning more to its European neighbours. New Zealand was going to have to stand more on its own. Labour's Prime Minister Kirk stated this new approach in a speech in 1973: *'From now on, when we have to deal with a new situation, we will not say, what do the British think about it [or] what would the Americans want us to do? Our starting point will be, what do we think about it?'*

THE FALKLAND WAR, 1982: NATIONAL

While Labour under Kirk in the early 1970s was looking to a more independent foreign policy, National in the early 1980s under Muldoon sought to rebuild links with Britain. Muldoon was quick to support Britain's 1982 war with Argentina over control of the remote Falkland Islands. As the crisis worsened, Muldoon broke off diplomatic relations with Argentina, before Britain had even requested it. He also made a New Zealand Navy ship available for Britain's use. Muldoon explained himself in an article written for the London *Times* newspaper, entitled 'Why We Stand With Our Mother Country.' Muldoon's enthusiasm to once more stand side by side with the 'Mother Country' came almost ten years after Britain had joined the European Economic Community, cutting its close ties with New Zealand. Muldoon's action was seen by many as out of step with a growing sense of an independent New Zealand identity.

ACTIVITIES

1 Refer to Source J

a In what part of Vietnam did the events described take place?

b Identify TWO facts in this source.

c Identify TWO opinions in this source.

d What is Doctor Smith's view of the war as whole? Provide evidence for your answer.

e Give TWO ways in which civilians from either side in the conflict were affected by the war.

f How might a supporter of the war respond to the incident in Source J?

g Why is this source on its own not enough to get a good understanding of the effects of the war on civilians?

2 Refer to Source K

a Identify ONE opinion in the source.

b Provide TWO separate facts that support the claim that the protest actions in which Shadbolt took part were not well supported.

c Provide evidence to support the claim that the American military had a presence in New Zealand.

3 Refer to Source L

How would the sort of events described in Source J and Source K lead to the Conference shown in Source L?

4 Re-read the 'Aftermath' section, page 30. Draw and label pictorials that show the three general areas of agreement on foreign policy between National and Labour.

5 Refer to page 28. Create two star diagrams. One should show the reasons that persuaded or pressured the Holyoake government into publicly supporting America in the Vietnam War. The second should show why privately Holyoake wanted to limit involvement.

6 What did Holyoake discover was the 'down-side' of being allied to America?

7 Sort the following key ideas about Labour's policies (page 30) into the correct order.

a Protests and demonstrations grow

b Labour calls for SEATO to focus on social and economic goals

c Kirk criticises US bombing of North Vietnam

d Kirk calls for the withdrawal of NZ troops.

e Labour establishes links with China and Russia.

f Labour becomes the government

g Labour says use the Commonwealth and UN.

h Labour reluctantly supports sending non-combat units

i Labour withdraws remaining troops.

8 Why was Muldoon's action over the Falklands seen by many as out of step with a growing sense of an independent New Zealand identity?

SOURCE J

'Had a three-year old die on me today. She came in with her guts torn apart by a grenade. Her mother, just a girl really, was with the child all the time, helping us to try and save her, and it was not until the child had died that we realised that the mother too had several wounds herself. The terrible sight of the dying child in the arms of the injured mother was most upsetting. It is horrible to think that our own troops will be inflicting the same sort of wounds on the same sort of people.'

Part of Dr Peter Smith's report in March 1969. Smith was the leader of a voluntary civilian surgical team, based at Qui Nhon hospital in South Vietnam.

SOURCE K

'The emphasis was on small but persistent action. Guerrilla protest. Pickets, leaflets, posters, parades. We were hounded and persecuted by police and public alike. Three times during the year I was assaulted. One guy spat in my face, another time about six clean-shaven rugby types surrounded me and started taunting.... We used to have marches down Queen Street. Our biggest rallies drew as many as 35 people. On one occasion we had six.... We also picketed American warships.... An Auckland housewife was arrested for singing anti-war songs on an American ship and was charged with offensive behaviour.'

Tim Shadbolt recalls early anti-Vietnam War protest action in 1968. (Shadbolt went on to become Mayor of Waitemata and then Invercargill.)

SOURCE L

9 History road

This activity can be done individually on a double page in workbooks, or as a group activity on a larger sheet of paper.

Create a 'history road' showing the development of the New Zealand response to the Vietnam War.

- **a** Begin by identifying the key events on the 'road'. You can use your responses to the activities on page 31 to guide you, but you may wish to select only the most important.
  Start with the general agreement on foreign policy prior to the Vietnam War and go through to the election of the Labour government and its refusal to host the 1974 SEATO Council meeting in Wellington.
- **b** Identify events that are 'crisis points'. These can be sharp 'turns' in the road.
- **c** Begin your 'history road' in one corner and do a rough sketch laying out the key events. Each event should have a signpost, and pictorials should be added in.
  Where the government was faced with a decision, you can create crossroads (with appropriate signposts) or even separate 'side roads', in cases where Labour's view differed from the government's actions.
- **d** Do a good copy.

Extension

10 Imagine that you are going on a protest against the Vietnam War. Come up with ideas for banners or placards to take with you on the protest. Also, think up some chants that the crowd could say. You need to decide what are the key ideas that you wish to express. To be taken seriously, you need to state FACTS.

AS1.4 REVIEW ACTIVITY

In a paragraph of 100–150 words each, describe the perspectives (views) and actions (with an accompanying explanation) for the following:

1. Signing up to, and participating in, ANZAM
2. Signing up to, and participating in, ANZUS
3. Signing up to, and participating in, SEATO
4. Participating in the Vietnam War – National
5. Participating in the Vietnam War – Labour
6. Participating in the Vietnam War – the protest movement
7. Foreign policy in general – National (views only)
8. Foreign policy in general – Labour (views only)

AS1.5 ESSAY PRACTICE

Follow the steps on the inside back cover to write the following essay.

How did New Zealand attempt to achieve collective security between 1945 and 1955? Describe New Zealand's involvement with the UN during this period.

- UN membership; ANZAM; ANZUS; SEATO
- Collective security; Security Council and veto; Korean War

OR

What were the important features of new security arrangements New Zealand made in the period 1945–1955? Why did New Zealand governments enter these new security arrangements?

- UN membership; ANZAM; ANZUS; SEATO
- Threat of Japan; uncertainty with regard to Britain; collective security; 'domino theory'.

AS1.6 REVIEW ACTIVITIES

1 Refer to the overview at the start of this section. Use the ideas there and the headings in the text to create a mind-map OR structured overview that shows the experiences that led to the shaping of New Zealand identity up to (and including) the Vietnam War.

2 For each of the following, write a 100–150 word paragraph that describes actions taken by New Zealand to:

- participate in, and support, the Commonwealth up to 1955
- participate in, and support, the United Nations up to 1950
- join allies in collective security arrangements up to 1955.

3 For each of the following, write a 100–150 word paragraph that shows how over time New Zealand has developed its own views with regard to:

- participation in Commonwealth activities
- participation in United Nations' activities
- working with its allies in collective security arrangements up to 1975.

RUGBY AND RACISM: SPORTING CONTACTS WITH SOUTH AFRICA

In terms of AS1.5 (essay writing – cause/course/consequences of an historical development) and AS1.6 (experiences that led to the shaping of a New Zealand identity) there were a number of key developments associated with sporting contact with South Africa.

OVERVIEW

The 1981 Springbok rugby tour of New Zealand led to the greatest civil unrest the country had seen. It showed that there was deep division within New Zealand society, and that New Zealanders were not the happy-go-lucky people they had thought they were. Supporters of the tour were generally dedicated followers of rugby who believed that sport and politics should not mix. Opponents of the tour believed that it was immoral to allow racially-selected teams to come to New Zealand. They believed that doing so would send a message that New Zealand supported South Africa's racist policies. Ongoing sporting contact with South Africa thus brought to the surface race relations issues. The response of different governments to the issue of playing rugby against the Springboks had less to do with whether National or Labour was in power, and more to do with difficult political choices.

Sporting contacts with South Africa and its apartheid government became an international issue, involving the Commonwealth and even the United Nations. The growing world opposition to South Africa coincided with the election of National's Robert Muldoon as Prime Minister. Muldoon's determination to resist this international pressure saw New Zealand's international reputation sink to its lowest point ever.

EXTENSION READING

APARTHEID: A BRIEF OVERVIEW

In 1948 South Africa introduced its policy of apartheid. Officially it was a policy of 'separate but equal development' for whites and non-whites. The laws, however, made the majority non–white South Africans into second-class citizens. Inter-racial mixing of any sort was forbidden. This meant separate train carriages, buses, drinking fountains, park benches, toilets, stairways and other facilities. Non-whites were forcibly moved out of areas designated as white. Non-whites were not allowed to play in national sporting teams with whites, such as the Springbok rugby team. South Africa's government also made it clear that it did not want its white-only teams playing against other countries with non-white players.

As resistance within South Africa to the apartheid laws grew, so did police brutality. Many countries expressed outrage in 1960 when 69 unarmed black protesters were killed in the 'Sharpeville Massacre'. A further 236 were killed in the Soweto Riots of 1976. International pressure on South Africa to end its apartheid policy increased. A number of nations agreed to end all contact – including sporting contact – with South Africa, until its policy changed.

EXTENSION READING

'Civil War' Over a Game of Rugby?

To understand why emotions ran so high during the 1981 Springbok Tour it is necessary to look at the role of rugby in New Zealand. The game of rugby has been played in New Zealand since the 1860s. For many it was simply an enjoyable pastime. For the country's moral leaders it was also seen as a way of channelling the boisterous behaviour of men into a game with rules. By the early 20th century, as more children were beginning to attend secondary school, the game was becoming popular. In terms of Maori–Pakeha relations, rugby was one of the few areas where both races met on equal terms.

The 1905 tour by the All Blacks to Britain marked the beginning of a national obsession with rugby. The New Zealanders beat the English, Irish and Scots. They lost to Wales only because an All Black try was controversially disallowed. In total, the All Blacks scored 802 points and had only 22 scored against them. This team has been nicknamed 'The Originals.'

The national interest in the team's success was enormous. Huge crowds greeted the All Blacks upon their arrival home. Foremost amongst the crowd was the Premier [Prime Minister] Richard Seddon. He went so far as to claim that a photograph of the All Blacks should be hung in every school. This was but a taste of the glory that was to come. The next tour to Britain occurred in 1924 and the All Blacks won every game. This time the team was nicknamed 'The Invincibles'. For many people, the All Blacks' comprehensive victory proved the superiority of New Zealand over the 'Mother Country' Britain.

South Africa

Links with South Africa began with a Springbok tour to New Zealand in 1921. South Africans loved their rugby as much as New Zealanders did and a great rivalry developed. The 1921 tour included a match against a Maori team, which the Springboks won 9-8. One South African journalist was appalled that the Springboks should have to play a 'coloured' Maori team. He noted that the only thing worse than this was the enthusiastic support which the Pakeha crowd gave them. This was 'too much for the Springboks who [were] frankly disgusted.' Because of this view, Maori players were omitted from a tour to South Africa in 1928. When the Springboks returned in 1937 the Rugby Union decided not to field a Maori team.

Even after the introduction of the apartheid laws in South Africa, the NZ Rugby Union did not challenge the exclusion of Maori from tours involving the Springboks. In effect, South Africa had extended apartheid to New Zealand rugby. When Maori were excluded from a tour to South Africa in 1949, public protest was voiced. Some people pointed with disgust to the similarities between the racial policy of apartheid and that of the Nazis. The President of the Returned Services Association, Sir Howard Kippenberger, expressed strong opposition on behalf of the soldiers who had died fighting Nazism. World War II had begun to change views on racial issues.

Crowd of rugby spectators in the rain at Athletic Park, Wellington 1921. There is confusion over how the name 'All Blacks' became attached to the New Zealand national team. Some sources say that it arose after an 1888 tour by a Maori team to England. Some suggest that it should really have been 'All Backs' because the back line was particularly skilful. The best explanation seems to be that it was simply because of the colour of the players' jerseys.

EXTENSION ACTIVITY

On a FULL page create a timeline from the information in the text that shows the key points in the development of sporting contacts with South Africa. Include at least the following (with pictorials):

- The developing role of rugby in New Zealand society
- Sporting links with South Africa
- Developments in South Africa's apartheid policy (1948, 1960, 1976)

1960: 'NO MAORIS, NO TOUR'

When the Rugby Union announced in 1959 that no Maori would be included in the team to tour South Africa in 1960, public protest grew dramatically. New Zealand rugby, for the sake of playing their great rivals, was again prepared to extend apartheid to the All Blacks. The Citizens' All Black Tour Association was formed to lead the protest. A petition with 156,000 signatures (many of whom were Pakeha) was presented to parliament urging that the tour be cancelled.

The All Black authority, T.P. McLean, initially supported the 1960 tour, but changed his mind. 'If it were not good enough for Maoris, with all their great contributions to rugby and the development of New Zealand as a nation, to be invited to South Africa as part of a rugby team, it was not good enough for the team to go.'

The Labour government was aware of the risk of losing votes at the 1959 election if it tried to stop the tour. It thus said that it had no power to interfere in the matter. Prime Minister Nash attempted to further justify his lack of action. He said that it was best that Maori did not go, as they would be offended by their treatment in South Africa. Some prominent Maori leaders publicly agreed with Nash. No politicians publicly condemned the tour, whatever their private feelings might have been. Only one Maori MP, Eruera Tirakatene, urged that the tour be cancelled, but even this protest was not made officially in parliament. Anti-tour demonstrations continued unsuccessfully, including a last-ditch attempt to stop the aircraft taking off. The All Blacks lost the test series. Some saw this as a just reward for omitting the Maori players. Labour also lost the 1960 election, although this had little to do with allowing the tour to proceed.

BACKGROUND TO THE 1981 SPRINGBOK TOUR

In the aftermath of the 'Sharpeville Massacre', international pressure went on South Africa, including a sporting boycott. This action was designed to target white South Africans only, for there were no mixed-race international teams. A tour of South Africa was planned for 1968, and the New Zealand Rugby Union again intended to exclude Maori. This time the government acted. In rejecting the tour, Prime Minister Holyoake said: 'as we are one people, we cannot be fully or truly represented by a team chosen on racial lines.' Rugby supporters, including many Maori, were deeply disappointed. Under pressure, South Africa modified its policy and allowed Maori to be included in a tour in 1970. It rather bizarrely classified Maori as 'honorary whites'.

South Africa's actions did not quieten the protesters. A *complete* sporting ban on South Africa was called for. Maori protest groups were in the forefront, as was the mainly Pakeha group, the Citizens' Association for Racial Equality (CARE). CARE also widened its protest beyond sporting contacts with South Africa to include debate upon the inferior position of Maori in New Zealand. Many of the different protest groups eventually came under the umbrella group HART (Halt All Racial Tours). All of these groups together did not, however, represent the majority view. An opinion poll taken in 1972 showed that 80% of New Zealanders supported the tour scheduled for 1973.

The build-up for the Springbok tour to New Zealand coincided with the 1972 election. Norman Kirk, the Labour leader, knew that his party would lose if they said that they would stop the tour. Kirk thus allowed the public to get the impression that a Labour government would not interfere. Labour won the election. As the prospect of the 1973 tour came closer, the police advised the government that violence would likely break out between pro- and anti-tour groups. The government put pressure on the Rugby Union to cancel the tour, but in the end Kirk had to cancel it himself. One of the reasons was that the Commonwealth Games were due to be held in Christchurch in 1974. Kirk did not want to risk having countries **boycott** the Games because New Zealand had allowed the tour. He was accused by rugby supporters of breaking his word.

The Muldoon Government

Rugby and South Africa again played a part in the 1975 election, and this time Robert Muldoon's National party won. In line with his party's policy, Muldoon refused to prevent a 1976 tour by the All Blacks to South Africa. International opinion now swung against New Zealand. Concerns were voiced in the Commonwealth and United Nations. Muldoon, however, was prepared to go against world opinion. New Zealand's international reputation hit its lowest point that year. Thirty countries, including twelve black African states, boycotted the Montreal Olympics. This was because a New Zealand team was attending. Some countries even talked of evicting New Zealand from the Commonwealth, as had happened to South Africa itself (South Africa had actually left just before being thrown out). Muldoon now realised that New Zealand was too small to resist international pressure. However, he was still not prepared to give in entirely. This made him popular with the many pro-Tour supporters.

Robert Muldoon

In 1977 the Commonwealth Heads of Government meeting was held in Gleneagles, Scotland. Attempts were made there to clarify the Commonwealth position on sporting links with South Africa. Muldoon resisted signing up to a declaration that committed New Zealand to ending such links. The watered-down final version of the 'Gleneagles Agreement' stated that countries would 'vigorously ... combat the evil of apartheid ... each government to determine, *in accordance with its laws*, the methods by which it might best discharge these commitments.' Because New Zealand had no laws forbidding sporting contact with South Africa, the Agreement did not *oblige* the government to do anything.

TIMELINE ACTIVITY

For those who have done the Extension timeline activity already, this timeline can follow on from it.

On a FULL page create a timeline from the information in the text that shows the key points in the development of opposition to sporting contacts with South Africa. Include at least the following (with pictorials):

- 3–4 points about the 1960 tour
- 1968
- The establishment of protest groups
- 1970
- 1973 proposed tour, including the background to it
- 1976 tour, including the background to it, and consequences of it
- 1977 – Gleneagles Agreement.

Demonstrators outside the South African Consulate, Wellington, in November 1977.

AS1.2 ACTIVITY – PROVIDE SUPPORTING EVIDENCE

Provide evidence from the text to support each of the following key ideas. (Evidence can include facts, quotes, statistics or similar.)

1. In 1960, public protest increased.
2. Prime Minister Nash took no real action to stop the 1960 Tour by the Springboks.
3. There was almost no criticism of the 1960 Tour by politicians.
4. Prime Minister Holyoake was opposed to racially selected teams and rejected a 1968 Tour.
5. A number of protest organisations were formed to oppose sporting links with South Africa.
6. By the 1972 election anti-Tour protesters were still a relatively small minority.
7. Prime Minister Kirk took into account several factors in making the decision to cancel the 1973 Springbok Tour.
8. Muldoon's support of the 1976 Tour had international consequences for New Zealand.
9. The Commonwealth was concerned about the issue of sporting contacts with South Africa.

THE 1981 SPRINGBOK TOUR

When the New Zealand Rugby Union proposed an eight-week tour by the Springboks, scheduled for July 1981, the Muldoon government followed its obligations under the Gleneagles Agreement. Rugby officials were contacted and informed that the government disapproved, but would not intervene to stop the tour. Muldoon said he supported the idea of '**bridge-building**' with South Africa. By this he meant showing South Africa, through continued contact, how a multi-racial country like New Zealand could have good race relations. According to Muldoon, this would encourage South Africa to change its ways.

The public, however, increasingly disagreed with Muldoon's view. A poll in May 1981 showed that 43% of people opposed the tour, with 41% in favour. (By the end of the tour the figures were 54% against and 42% for.) In terms of protest action, there had been the anti-Vietnam War demonstrations in the 1960s and early 1970s, but nothing like the violence of the Springbok Tour. In some cases, families were bitterly divided between pro- and anti-tour support. The issue polarised the wider community too, with few people not having a view one way or the other.

Protest groups took an organised approach, working out tactics in advance. To counter them, specially trained police were formed into the Riot Squad, the first such force in New Zealand. To counter the Riot Squad's aggressive approach, front-line protesters donned crash helmets and padded clothing. Some carried shields, on occasions with spikes imbedded in them. Dedicated protesters would sometimes travel great distances to be present at demonstrations. At some rugby fields, barricades of barbed wire were erected by the army. Shipping containers were also brought in to block demonstrators' access to the playing field.

Over the eight weeks of disturbances nearly 2000 New Zealanders were arrested. The second game (at Hamilton) was cancelled after protesters occupied the field, possibly scattering tacks and glass. A light aircraft buzzed the seating stands, the pilot's intentions unknown. After the protesters had been escorted off the field by the police, rugby supporters attacked them. A game at Timaru was also cancelled for security reasons. At the final test in Auckland a protester dressed as the referee ran onto the field and stole the ball. The game went ahead, with some 10,000 protesters outside the grounds. Also outside the grounds was the Riot Squad. Charge and counter-charge by police and protesters alike saw some of the bloodiest scenes of the tour. A light aircraft again buzzed the field, this time dropping flour bombs and flares onto the pitch below. All these images were relayed on national and international television.

Aftermath

The 1981 Springbok Tour left the country divided like it had never been before. With the election of David Lange's Labour government in 1984 there would be no further tours. In reaction to Labour's stance, the South Africans closed their Embassy in Wellington. Despite the Labour government's position, the Rugby Union proposed a tour of South Africa in 1985. In the end it was actually Court action by two University players that prevented it. Apartheid in South Africa collapsed in 1990. Nelson Mandela, the new black South African leader, acknowledged New Zealand's role in helping to force this change. In New Zealand, the Tour raised many questions for Maori activists. Why, they asked, had so many protesters risked arrest or physical harm to support people in a country thousands of miles away, when Maori were facing injustice in their own country, even if it was not on the same scale?

ACTIVITIES

1. Explain what Prime Minister Muldoon meant by 'bridge-building'.
2. Provide evidence to support the claim that by the time of the 1981 Springbok Tour a majority of New Zealanders were opposed to it.
3. Describe briefly the approach of both protesters and police to the increasing confrontations.

AS1.2 ACTIVITY – IDENTIFY KEY IDEAS

Refer to the text on page 37

From the list below, select only what you think are the SIX key ideas. For each, draw an appropriate pictorial.

1 Rugby officials were contacted.
2 Muldoon's government went through the motions.
3 Muldoon's government did not stop the 1981 Tour.
4 The anti-Tour movement prepared for action.
5 There had been public protest during the Vietnam War.
6 The Tour caused deep division within New Zealand.
7 Nearly 2000 protesters were arrested.
8 No further Tours occurred after Labour came to power.
9 Maori activists had many questions after the Tour.
10 Maori activists pointed out the contradiction in many New Zealanders views/actions.
11 Anti-Tour protests had been a part of the pressure that saw apartheid collapse in South Africa by 1990.
12 The injustices Maori said they faced in New Zealand were on a lesser scale than those in South Africa.

ACTIVITIES

Refer to Source A

1 What is it that the protester in the cartoon wants?

2 What organisation is represented by the protester?

3 Is the cartoonist critical or supportive of this organisation and its goals? Explain your answer.

4 How might the organisation itself respond to this cartoon?

Refer to Source B

5 What aspects of the poster indicate that it has been produced in response to New Zealand playing rugby with South Africa?

6 What immediate action does the poster call for?

7 What organisation produced the poster? What is its attitude towards sporting links with South Africa? Explain your answer.

8 What is the link between the cartoon (Source A) and the poster (Source B)?

ACTIVITIES

Refer to Source C

9 Why is the crowd protesting? Provide evidence to support your answer.

10 What does the Minister of Police mean when he says "lyin' commy" (see page 8)? How does this statement fit into the foreign policy ideas studied earlier in this course?

11 What is the cartoonist's attitude towards the Minister of Police? Explain your answer.

12 How useful is this Source on its own to the historian trying to understand the issues surrounding the 1981 Springbok Tour?

SOURCE C

SOURCE D

Refer to Source D

13 What organisation is referred to in the poster as 'New Zealand's top street gang'?

14 Is this poster likely to have been produced by a pro- or anti-Tour group? Explain your answer.

15 Explain the common link between this source and Source C.

16 How does the police response as shown in Source D compare to the sort of protester shown in Source A? Which poster do you feel more accurately reflects what actually happened during the Tour? Explain your answer.

SOURCE E

Refer to Source E

17 In your own words, what is it that the poster wants people to do in order to 'stop the Tour'?

18 What is the *visual* link between this source and Source B?

19 How does this source show that New Zealand is in danger from the Tour?

20 What might be the link between this source and Source A?

EXTENSION READING

The 1981 Springbok Tour: Different Perspectives

SOURCE F

'By this time the Wellington game of the Tour was fast approaching. I was by now quite skilled at padding my chest and shoulders, and on the day of the match, I set out wearing Mark's crash helmet ... [*The protesters then entered the playing field before the game, but were moved off by the police.*] We finally hit the road and started back to town. On the way we passed a pub where rugby fans who hadn't been able to get into the park had been watching the match on television. They poured out of the pub and assailed us, threw beer cans, and a young Maori man spat in my face. Someone saw a man he knew behind me and lashed out with a punch. Unfortunately he missed and punched me very hard, catching me below my padding.'

Sonia Davies was 58 when she participated in this anti-Tour protest. The blow she received broke three ribs and cracked two others.

SOURCE G

'After the game was officially called off the police had the job to escort the hard-core protesters from the field. Their selected route was in the corner between our stand and the long, low touchline stand. The police had to cordon off both sides of the path out. As rugby fans' communal anger boiled over there were two distinct crowd rushes toward the departing protesters, and mayhem ensued. Through gaps in the police line the protesters were kicked, punched, cursed and spat at by rugby 'hooligans' – a priest-protester was punched and the nearest line-cop turned around quickly and said to the puncher: "If you do that again, I'll kick your f...ing head in." This fighting carried on spasmodically outside the ground into the evening. All of NZ was shocked at this first 'heavy' confrontation over the 'Tour', with the police trying to be the barrier between two committed factions – showing up real divisions in NZ society.'

A rugby supporter recalls the aftermath of the cancellation of the Hamilton game.

SOURCE H

'All the training, all the planning now came into focus ... this final showdown was the battle that had to be fought. Those opposing us were the protesters that had chosen of their own free will to take the police head on .... We would, in a disciplined, professional and positive manner, maintain the rule of law and defeat those who sought to bring anarchy to the streets .... At first we were pelted with rocks, bottles, cans and several incendiary [fire] devices, two of which had to be extinguished. The [Red] Squad smashed its way through what had seemed an impenetrable wall of shields and was, for a few moments, forced to baton down on those in front to stop the momentum of the mob. But within minutes the superior fortitude [courage] of the few overcame the brute force of the many and the tide began to turn with the relentlessness of our advance ...'

Ross Meurant was second-in-command of a police riot team known as the Red Squad. The events described occurred at the final Springbok match at Auckland.

SOURCE I

Julie and Murray Kilpatrick wrote protest songs during the violence of the 1981 Springbok tour. These are some of the verses.

When you're marching in the protest and you're heading for the game
And in front of you's the Red Squad not looking very tame
And behind you are the Blue Squad and you're wondering why you came
Well don't worry mate, she'll be right. She'll be right mate ...
Just duck and run for cover, they'll do battle with each other
So don't worry mate, she'll be right.

The coppers swing their batons, just like a bloody mace.
So I went and bought a helmet for protection for me face.
Now I have the feeling I'm protecting the wrong place.
Well don't worry mate, she'll be right. She'll be right mate ...
Take your helmet off your head, put it lower down instead.
And don't worry mate, she'll be right.

EXTENSION

Refer to the text and Sources A–I.

1. Imagine that you are going on a protest against the Springbok Tour. In your exercise book, come up with ideas for banners or placards to take with you on the protest. Also, think up some chants that the crowd could say.
   - You need to decide what the key ideas are that you wish to express.
   - To be taken seriously, you need to state FACTS.
2. Write a letter to the editor of a newspaper outlining thoughtfully the reasons for your opposition to – OR support for – the 1981 Springbok Tour. Include factual material to back up your point of view.
3. Create a sketch of a 'typical' confrontation between police and protesters.
4. Create a plan for an anti-tour protest action – OR for the police tactics to be used to counter a protest. Include a sketch of the rugby grounds, showing roads and any barriers, and where you and your 'side' will station yourselves.

AS1.4 REVIEW ACTIVITY

In a paragraph of 100–150 words each, describe the perspectives (views) and actions (with an accompanying explanation) for the following:

1. Prime Minister Keith Holyoake and the 1968 tour to South Africa
2. Prime Minister Norman Kirk and the 1973 tour to South Africa
3. Prime Minister Robert Muldoon and sporting contact with South Africa
4. The Commonwealth Heads of Government and sporting contact with South Africa
5. Black African Commonwealth nations and sporting contact with South Africa
6. Pro-Tour supporters and the 1981 Springbok Tour
7. Anti-Tour protesters (Nga Tamatoa, CARE, HART) and the 1981 Springbok Tour.

AS1.6 REVIEW ACTIVITY

1. Refer to the overview at the start of this section. Use the ideas there and the headings in the text to create a mind-map OR structured overview that shows the experiences that led to the shaping of New Zealand's identity up to (and including) the 1981 Springbok Tour.
2. For both points below, write a 100-150 word paragraph.
   - Describe actions taken by the Muldoon government from 1975–1981 with regard to sporting contacts with South Africa.
   - Show how over time opposition within New Zealand to sporting contacts with South Africa developed (up to 1981).

AS1.5 ESSAY PRACTICE

Follow the steps outlined on the inside back cover to write the following essay.

What events led to division in New Zealand over the issue of sporting contact with South Africa up to the 1960s? How did the different sides respond to the issue up to 1981?

- role of rugby in New Zealand; South Africa's apartheid policy; exclusion of Maori from Tours.
- protest organisations CARE and HART; Labour; National; public protest over the 1981 Tour.

CHAPTER SIX

NEW ZEALAND AND PACIFIC ISLAND NATIONS

In terms of AS1.5 (essay writing – cause/course/consequences of an historical development) and AS1.6 (experiences that led to the shaping of a New Zealand identity) there were a number of key developments in New Zealand's relationship with the Pacific.

OVERVIEW

Before WWII, New Zealand had been somewhat high-handed in its dealings with the Pacific Islands under its authority. After WWII, and with Labour in power, New Zealand took its responsibilities more seriously. This was for several reasons. The first was because of a commitment to the United Nations' programme of decolonisation. This meant self-government for all peoples who wanted it. Second, there was a growing belief that improving the living conditions of people was the best defence against communism or revolution. Third, by taking on its share of responsibilities in the region, it would (it was believed) encourage Britain to stay.

New Zealand's role in the Pacific thus evolved into one of both partner and protector. Through Pacific organisations such as the Pacific Forum, leaders in the region were able to meet and discuss problems. New Zealand (and other Pacific area nations) also made available police and peacekeepers when asked, or when potential threats arose. However, the limits of the power of New Zealand and the other main Pacific nation, Australia, were made clear during the Fiji coups.

Two other important aspects of New Zealand's relationship with the Pacific were immigration and aid. Pacific Island people with historical links to New Zealand were eligible to emigrate to New Zealand and, from the 1960s, many did so. While this filled a labour shortage at the time, adjustment to the urban New Zealand lifestyle was not easy. When the economy faltered in the early 1970s, the new migrants were made to feel far less welcome. Another significant contribution to the Pacific was aid. Some of this came through direct funding of projects, while in other cases technical support or training was provided. Despite the fact that New Zealand's greatest aid contribution was to the Pacific, the government never met the overall level required by its UN obligations.

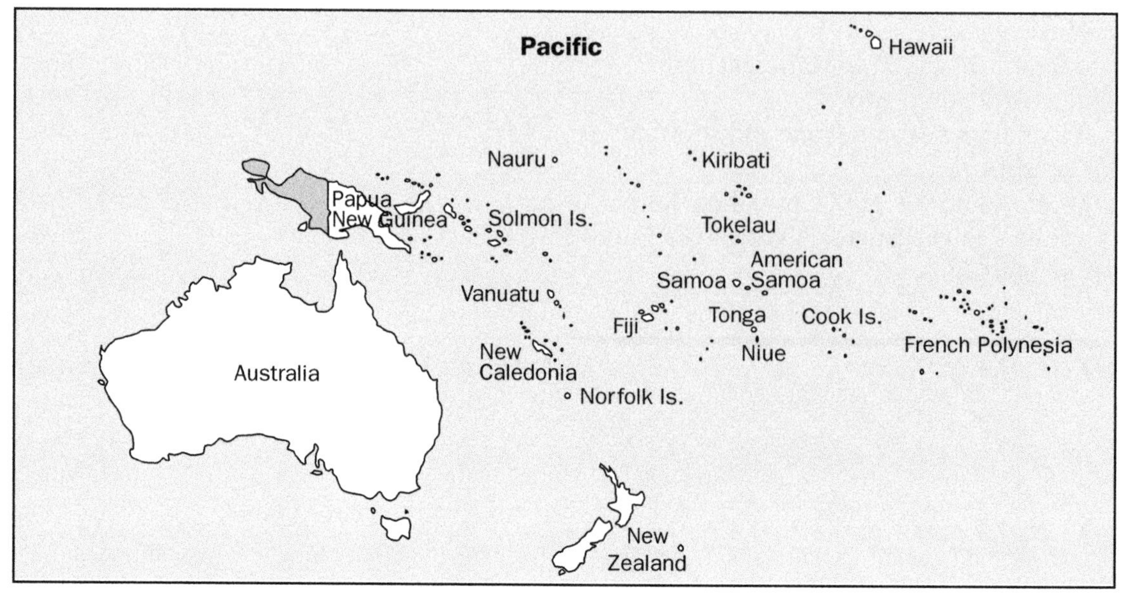

New Zealand's 'Pacific Empire'

New Zealand's interest in the Pacific extends back to the 19th century. Under politicians such as 'King Dick' Seddon, New Zealand looked to establish its own 'Pacific Empire'. In 1901, Britain finally agreed to place the Cook Islands and Niue under New Zealand's control. Like other politicians before him, Seddon wanted more. Calls had already been made for Norfolk Island, Samoa, Fiji, and the Society Islands to become part of New Zealand's 'Pacific Empire'. Seddon had even suggested to the U.S. President that New Zealand should take over Hawaii. When WWI broke out in 1914, Western Samoa was a German colony. New Zealand troops were rapidly despatched and occupied the islands without a shot being fired.

A New Zealand gun crew on horseback. They were part of the occupying force in Samoa during WWI

After WWI the League of Nations granted New Zealand the mandate to rule Western Samoa. New Zealand's job was to prepare Western Samoa for eventual independence. New Zealand was also made responsible for Nauru, jointly with Australia. In 1923, Britain granted control of the Ross Dependency in Antarctica to New Zealand, and in 1925 Tokelau also came under New Zealand control.

Despite the expansion of New Zealand's 'Empire', there was at first little real New Zealand interest in helping Pacific Island nations to develop. In Western Samoa after WWI, there followed a period of heavy-handed New Zealand rule that saw the development of the nationalist Mau movement.

Mau prisoners caught in a crackdown on the nationalist organisation

The low-point of New Zealand's administration came with the shooting of eleven Samoan protesters in 1929. Later, during the Japanese advances of WWII, the South Pacific became more important to New Zealand, especially as the United States took a greater role in the area. After the war was over, however, New Zealand's main concern was to assist Britain to re-establish and maintain its presence in the Pacific/South East Asia area. Nonetheless, New Zealand took its own Pacific responsibilities seriously, more especially when Britain withdrew from the region in the early 1970s.

'Black Sunday' Mau parade in Apia Samoa, December 1929

ACTIVITY

Place these background events on a timeline that shows the changing relationship between New Zealand and the Pacific.

DECOLONISATION

Decolonisation is the process whereby European colonial powers prepared the native people of a country to govern themselves, eventually resulting in full independence. As part of its support for the United Nations, New Zealand also supported the process of decolonisation. After WWII, New Zealand had accepted the UN Trusteeship of Western Samoa. The aim was to help that country prepare itself for self-government. In 1962, Western Samoa became independent and, later that year, signed with New Zealand a Treaty of Friendship. By agreement, New Zealand remained responsible for Western Samoa's defence and international relations, other than in the Pacific. Six years later, Nauru became independent. In 1970 Britain withdrew from its responsibilities in the Pacific, when both Tonga and Fiji became fully independent.

The Queen of Tonga inspects her soldiers.

New Zealand's process of Pacific decolonisation was entirely peaceful, despite the dire warning of Indonesian President Sukarno. In 1965 he had stated that the people 'to our east in Oceania must be given a chance to become masters in their own homes and manage their own affairs ... do not be shocked if a time comes when the Pacific Ocean explodes, rebels, and the peoples set up their own independent countries.' This was truer of the French experience, where violent uprisings ended their rule in Africa and Asia. Increasingly violent protest by the Kanaks also occurred in New Caledonia from 1984. By contrast, some Pacific nations even chose to retain their links to New Zealand. Both the Cook Islands (1965) and Niue (1974) opted for self-government in 'free association' with New Zealand. This meant that New Zealand shared some responsibility for these Island nations' international affairs. Tokelau refused even this form of independence. All three nations retained some citizenship rights in New Zealand.

One way in which New Zealand maintained an interest in the Pacific Islands was through the South Pacific Commission (SPC). This was an organisation set up in 1947 through the Canberra Pact. Its goal was to improve living conditions for Pacific Island nations. Britain, Australia, the United States, France and Holland – all nations that had territories in the region – were also involved. By the early 1970s, the SPC had been virtually replaced by the Pacific Forum. The Pacific nations themselves played a more prominent part in the Forum.

A NEW PACIFIC ROLE

New Zealand's relationship with the South Pacific became closer from the 1970s. New Zealand's reluctant involvement in the Vietnam War had made it careful about being caught up again in an Asian war. In addition, despite New Zealand's wishes, Britain continued to reduce its commitments in the Pacific. New Zealand felt obliged to step in and maintain stability in the region. It set out to do this by developing a new role in the Pacific, based on partnership.

An indication of the desire for a more active partnership with Pacific leaders was the formation in 1971 of the Pacific Forum. This came about in part due to the frustration of Pacific leaders with European dominance of the South Pacific Commission (SPC). With the establishment of the Pacific Forum, the SPC gradually became less relevant. By the end of the century, the seven founding members of the Forum (New Zealand, Australia, Cook Islands, Fiji, Nauru, Tonga and Western Samoa) had been joined by nine others. Although Australia and New Zealand dominated the Forum in terms of economic power, all member nations met as equals. The informal style of meetings, and decision-making by general agreement, became known as the 'Pacific Way'. An important goal of the Forum was to try to improve the economic situation of Pacific nations. One main step towards this was the formation of the Pacific Forum Shipping Line in 1978. This was set up in order to make the import and export of goods easier throughout the Pacific.

Pacific Security

As well as development issues, security in the Pacific region was of some concern. New Zealand provided direct assistance to the Cook Islands in 1978. This came after a request for police to be sent to help maintain law and order when a dispute over an election result threatened to escalate into violence. The Cold War and the risk of terrorism also intruded into the Pacific. Vanuatu had become independent from France in 1980, as a result of pressure from a nationalist movement. In the early 1980s Vanuatu seemed prepared to allow Soviet interests to operate from its territory. The Pacific Forum made its opposition clear, and Vanuatu backed down.

Also of concern to Forum members was Kanak nationalist pressure in French-ruled New Caledonia. This was especially so when links were detected with the Soviet Union and Libya, a 'terrorist State'. In response to this, the Forum considered developing a military Ready Reaction Force that could operate wherever needed in the Pacific. Although this idea did not go any further, New Zealand's military was heavily involved in 1997 in negotiating peace between the island of Bougainville, and Papua New Guinea. New Zealand peacekeepers also took a prominent role in East Timor from 1999. (The New Zealand government had not, however, taken any action when Indonesian troops first occupied East Timor in 1975.)

ACTIVITIES

Refer to the text in this section and use FULL answers for the following questions.

1. What was the goal of the United Nations' Trusteeship programme? How did this affect New Zealand?
2. How did New Zealand's decolonisation process compare to that of France? Give examples to back up your answer.
3. Draw diagrams or pictorials showing New Zealand's relationship with the Pacific nations of Western Samoa, Niue, the Cook Island and Tokelau as a result of the decolonisation process.
4. Provide evidence to back up the claim that former colonial powers such as Britain, France, NZ, Holland, the U.S. and Australia maintained an interest in the Pacific after decolonisation.
5. Why was the Pacific Forum created, and what was its purpose?
6. In terms of the Pacific Forum, what does 'Pacific Way' mean?
7. In what ways has New Zealand been involved in the Pacific in terms of security issues since decolonisation?

SOURCE A

'It will continue to be of overriding importance for New Zealand that the South Pacific generally should remain Western-oriented ... to avoid the development of conditions of political or economic instability which the Soviet Union or some other unfriendly or opportunistic power could exploit [and] to ensure that the western powers themselves ... are responsive to South Pacific concerns'.

An official from New Zealand's Ministry of Foreign Affairs

Refer to Source A

8. How useful is this source to an historian wanting to find out about New Zealand's policy in the Pacific? Explain your answer.
9. Under what conditions does the speaker believe that the Soviet Union could become involved in the Pacific?
10. Does the speaker feel Soviet involvement in the Pacific would be a desirable thing or not? Provide evidence to support your answer.

THE FIJI COUPS

A serious security issue arose in Fiji in 1987 when a military coup toppled the elected government. The background to the coup was tension between native Fijians and Indo-Fijians. Indians had been brought into Fiji from the late 19th century by the British government to work the sugarcane plantations. Many chose to stay and, due to rapid population growth, by WWII there were slightly more Indo-Fijians than native Fijians. When Fiji became independent from Britain in 1970 there was concern amongst native Fijians. They feared that they would come under the control of an Indo-Fijian dominated government. This did in fact occur in 1987, although the newly-elected government stressed that it would preserve native Fijian interests. This was not good enough for Fijian nationalists, including sections of the Army. The coup, led by Colonel Sitiveni Rabuka, created great difficulties for New Zealand. What was the appropriate response to a military takeover? The Lange government was quick to defend democratic principles by condemning the coup. Other Pacific leaders – and Maori in New Zealand – were more cautious. Some even voiced support of the action, claiming that the native Fijians were right to take action to protect their heritage. In the end, neither New Zealand nor Australia did anything more than vigorously protest. Military action had been ruled out early on, partly because the Fijian Army was a well-trained fighting force – thanks to New Zealand. Furthermore, the use of force – even against an illegal military coup – was not considered to be the 'Pacific Way'. Fiji was, however, evicted from the Commonwealth. This affair showed the limitations of the power of New Zealand (and Australia) in the Pacific.

Colonel Sitiveni Rabuka

New Zealand was more involved in the process of trying to bring stability and democracy back to Fiji. A former New Zealand Governor-General, Sir Paul Reeves, was invited to be part of a three-man Commission responsible for writing a new Fijian Constitution. This was a difficult task, for the democratic rights of the Indo-Fijians had to be balanced against native Fijian concerns about loss of power in their own country. Finally, in 1997 the new Constitution was released and Fiji was readmitted to the Commonwealth. In 1999, the first election under the new Constitution took place. The following year, as tension increased, another coup occurred, led by George Speight. Although democracy was eventually returned to Fiji, the underlying issues were not resolved. Furthermore, each coup resulted in large numbers of Indo-Fijians abandoning their country of birth. Many of those who left were well-educated, thus creating more problems for Fiji.

IMMIGRATION

Relations between New Zealand and some other Pacific countries were also occasionally strained. One issue that created some ill-feeling was immigration. As noted above, Niue, the Cook Islands and Western Samoa had relatively free access to New Zealand. During the 1960s, many Pacific Islanders were encouraged to migrate to help fill an industrial labour shortage in this country. By the 1970s, as economic conditions worsened, calls came from different sectors of New Zealand society to stop immigration from the Pacific. In 1975, National looked at the idea of deporting lawbreaking immigrants. This shows that in some people's minds, immigration was linked to crime. Immigration regulations, and the policing of them, were tightened. In 1976, the infamous 'Dawn Raids' occurred. Police would call at houses in the early morning, hoping to catch suspected overstayers. This caused an outcry from Pacific Island leaders. Furthermore, the fact that a number of Maori had been caught up in the 'raids' caused accusations of racism. The following year, the Minister responsible for the Pacific made the first-ever comprehensive tour of the Pacific in an effort to smooth relations.

ACTIVITIES

1 Use the following key ideas to write a brief summary of the issue of Pacific immigration. Be sure to add at least one fact or detail for each point given.

- Industrial labour shortage
- Deteriorating economic conditions
- Immigration-crime link
- 'Dawn Raids'
- Accusations of racism

Refer to Source B

2 According to the pamphlet, what are the main differences between Pakeha and Polynesians with regard to character and money?

3 Identify the facts in these extracts.

4 What, according to this source, *seems* to be the cause of Pakeha finding it 'hard to relax' and thus needing 'a little alcohol' to loosen them up?

5 How useful is this source to the historian in helping understand the problems facing new immigrants from the Pacific? Explain your answer.

Kirikiti in Island Bay Wellington

SOURCE B

The following extracts are from *Understanding Pakehas*, published by the Polynesian Advisory Committee in 1978. It was a booklet produced to help recent immigrants from the Pacific Islands to adjust to life in New Zealand.

Pakeha Character: Individualistic

Everything in Western society emphasises the individual. In religion, every person has to find his own salvation. In politics, each person is expected to make his views known. With Polynesians, it is the family which gives a person status and position. With Pakehas, each has to make his own way in the world and win status by what he succeeds in doing and owning. In many instances, therefore, Pakehas put the individual before the group, the self before the others.

Pakeha Character: Money-Minded

A Polynesian knows that he can depend on his relatives in time of need because they share what they have with him. Your family is your security, and the more there are, the better. A Pakeha cannot depend on his relatives to the same extent. Usually he alone must be responsible for keeping his wife and children.... He has also been brought up to be proud of his ability to provide for himself and his family without relying on others.

Social Drinks

When Pakehas get together with friends for a chat, they like to have a few drinks. This is because many Pakehas find it hard to relax and a little alcohol helps them loosen up. So they drink in order to be sociable, not to get drunk.... Often, however, Pakehas get drunk in pubs and at parties. Although they may not intend to get drunk, this happens because so much drink is available in these places. If you are not used to alcohol, it is better not to follow their example, as you may do something you would not normally do or approve of.

Asian Immigration

As the Vietnam War drew to a close in the early 1970s, New Zealand's links with South East Asia diminished. In 1989, the last military link was cut as troops were withdrawn from their base in Singapore. As New Zealand's foreign policy began to focus on the Pacific, immigration policy began to widen to include Asia. This was a significant change from earlier times.

Non-European migration to New Zealand was restricted up until the end of WWII. Since the late 19th century there had been an unofficial 'White New Zealand' immigration policy. It was believed that New Zealand's future was to be the 'Britain of the South Seas'. To limit the numbers of 'aliens' coming into the country, Chinese had to pay a special tax. This policy was so effective that by the time it was abolished in 1944, there were fewer than 5000 Chinese in New Zealand. (New Zealand was the last Commonwealth country to get rid of such restrictions.) Most of the Chinese here at that time were in fact New Zealand born. The other main non-white group was Indians, with about 1500 in 1945. They were exposed to the same sort of discriminatory laws as the Chinese.

The main changes in immigration policy came about because of economic reasons, rather than a change in racial attitudes. During the 1970s and into the 1980s, New Zealand's economy went into serious decline. Many New Zealanders left to seek better lives overseas, especially in Australia. A large number of these were skilled people, which left New Zealand even worse off. To counter the outward flow, the law was changed in 1987 to make skills, rather than nationality, the basis of immigration policy. In the 1990s another change introduced a system that favoured young people, investors, and those with professional qualifications. This change recognised the positive economic impact that immigration could have. By the end of the 20th century, New Zealand was again an 'immigrant nation', with nearly 20% of the population being overseas born.

The number of Asian migrants increased rapidly in the 1990s. By the year 2000 there were 240,000 people of Asian descent in New Zealand, slightly more than the entire Pacific Island population. Nationally, this represented over 6% of the total population. Two-thirds of the Asian immigrants were living in Auckland. The two largest groups of immigrants in 2000 were Chinese (8,700) and Indian (8,400) – well above the third placed United Kingdom (6,600) and fourth placed South Africa (4,300). Asian numbers were further boosted by a policy of promoting New Zealand as an educational destination. By the year 2000, there were 7,000 primary and 11,500 secondary Asian fee-paying students (not permanent). They contributed over $500million to the economy, making education the fourth largest export sector.

Despite this positive impact, some New Zealanders found it difficult to adjust to the 'sea' of new faces. There was a mixed reaction to Prime Minister Bolger's statement that New Zealand must view itself as part of Asia. Nonetheless, the National government helped establish Asia 2000, an organisation responsible for developing cultural and trade links with Asia. These efforts were not enough to calm the fears of those who felt overwhelmed by the suddenness of the changes. Cases of discrimination were not uncommon. One political party – New Zealand First – talked of an 'Asian invasion' and campaigned on an anti-immigration policy. By the end of the 1990s, many New Zealanders were still to come to terms with the fact that New Zealand was shifting 'from Empire to internationalism' – no longer was it the 'Britain of the South Seas'.

EXTENSION ACTIVITIES

Refer to the text on page 47

1. What policy meant that there were fewer than 5000 Chinese in New Zealand by 1945?
2. What were the main changes to immigration laws in the late 1980s and 1990s?
3. In what region was the effect of Asian immigration most noticeable? Provide evidence to support your answer.
4. Explain in your own words the term 'from Empire to internationalism'.

Refer to Source C

5. What key idea from the text do the figures from 1986 onwards support?

Refer to Source D

6. In what year was the largest loss of population?
7. Between what two consecutive years was there the single biggest change in net migration?
8. What key idea from the text about economic conditions do the figures up to 1982 support?

Refer to Source E

9. What key idea from the text does this cartoon support?

SOURCE C

Asian Immigration (includes Indians)	
Year	**Number**
1945	6500
1966	20,000
1986	54,000
1991	90,000
2000	240,000

SOURCE D

Net migration to NZ	
Year	**Net inflow**
1977	-16270
1978	-22156
1979	-26544
1980	-21314
1981	-16209
1982	-4743
1983	15442
1984	10557
1985	217
1986	-18518
1987	4357
1988	-957
1989	-18298
1990	-1633
1991	14576
1992	2938
1993	8080
1994	15793
1995	20401
1996	28626
1997	37779
1998	1923

SOURCE E

FOREIGN AID POLICY

New Zealand governments have seen the giving of aid as an important part of maintaining stability in various parts of the world. It was accepted that aid relieves poverty and helps poorer nations to develop self-sufficiency. New Zealand believed that people with a reasonable standard of living would not be influenced by 'radical' ideas such as communism or revolution. The giving of aid also improves the donor country's international reputation. In addition, aid has the advantage of helping poorer economies grow so that they can import New Zealand goods. Labour governments in particular have also talked about aid in humanitarian and moral terms: it is right to help those who need it.

The New Zealand government has provided aid in two main ways: bilateral and multilateral. Bilateral aid is assistance given *directly* to another country. It is often for a specific project, such as building a school, hospital or runway. Most of New Zealand's aid has been given in this way. Multilateral aid is assistance given through another organisation, such as the United Nations or the Commonwealth. New Zealand's first major multilateral commitment of foreign aid after WWII was through the Commonwealth. At a meeting in Colombo (Sri Lanka) in 1950 it was agreed to provide assistance to the countries of Asia, and in particular South East Asia. This was called the Colombo Plan.

Colombo Plan conference, Wellington, 1956.

One example of New Zealand's contribution was the sending of five Army Engineers to Thailand to help build a 144km-long sealed road. Another was the placement of students from countries such as Malaysia in New Zealand schools. Despite these efforts, New Zealand was slow to contribute the required aid money. The government claimed that economic problems made it difficult to do so.

NEW ZEALAND'S FOREIGN AID EFFORT

New Zealand's poor aid effort in the 1960s saw the emergence of a pressure group called the One Percent Aid movement. This group of concerned citizens, and organisations such as churches, demanded that New Zealand do better. Their call was for New Zealand to honour its United Nations commitment of giving 1% of the country's Gross National Product (GNP – the amount of wealth the country produces in any particular year). Under this promise, 70% of the total was to come from the government itself. The other 30% was to have come from private organisations. Although New Zealand funded a number of development projects, mostly in South East Asia, this target was never met. Instead of a government contribution of 0.7% GNP, the average through the 1960s and early 1970s was only 0.3% GNP. This was despite the National government making a large increase in aid in the late 1960s.

When the government changed during the 1970s, New Zealand's aid policy also changed. In 1973 at the United Nations, the new Labour Prime Minister, Norman Kirk, expressed his concerns about poverty. 'The fact that a vast gap exists between the rich nations and the poor nations and that it is widening not narrowing, is one of the great international issues – perhaps the greatest – of our time....' Kirk announced that his government would try to meet the UN requirements. By 1975 the level of government aid had risen to 0.6% GNP, the highest ever level. Furthermore, a greater amount of this aid was now being directed to Pacific Island nations. When National came to power later that year aid was reduced. Prime Minister Muldoon claimed that the country could not afford more.

By the 1990s New Zealand's aid contribution had slipped back below the levels of the 1970s. In 1999 New Zealand gave $253million in aid, a figure which was still only 0.27% of GNP. This equated to just under $67 per New Zealander, half of what Australians gave. It was also one of the lowest levels in the developed world. Nevertheless, Pacific Island nations continued to receive about 40% of New Zealand's total aid package, often through educational or technical services. The administration of overseas aid was reorganised in 1999 with the creation of a new aid agency, NZAid. (Information on agencies and organisations working on development projects in the Pacific can be found in the Pacific Development Directory.)

ACTIVITY

Foreign aid summary

The key ideas and examples below are from the text in this section. Copy out the table and use the text to help you fill in the gaps.

Use the completed table to write a one to two paragraph summary OR create pictorials to go with each box.

Foreign Aid Policy	New Zealand's Effort
Reasons: aid = stability Relieve ________ Encourage self-________ Prevent ________/communism Enhance donor's ________ Build ________ = more exports Labour = ________ and moral reasons	New Zealand's poor aid effort One ________ Aid ________ ____ commitment of ________ of GNP 1960s/70s average = ________ GNP
Bilateral aid ________ between countries Targeted to ________ projects Most NZ ________ given this way	New government = new policy Labour = slow ________ in aid given Increased amount to ________ National = ________ amount given
Multilateral aid Given via other ________ ________ Plan's focus on ________ Asia	1990s = poor effort Less than ________ level 1999 = ________ GNP One of the world's ________ levels Pacific = ________ of total

SOURCE F

Selected countries receiving official aid from New Zealand

Country/Amount	1988 ($million)	1990 ($million)	1992 ($million)	Aid received *per person* in each country
Cook Islands	14.1	14.1	14.3	$831
Niue	9.3	9.7	9.5	$4,850
Tokelau	4.7	4.7	5.0	$2,280
Tonga	4.1	4.1	4.3	$40
Tuvalu	1.7	1.7	1.8	$168
W. Samoa	5.7	5.7	6.0	$35

SOURCE G

Remittances (money sent 'home' by relatives living in New Zealand), 1990

Country	Amount ($million)
Cook Islands	6.0
Niue	2.0
Tokelau	1.0
Tonga	10.0
Tuvalu	No figures
W. Samoa	30.3

SOURCE H

Exports to New Zealand, 1990

Country	Amount ($million)
Cook Islands	3.9
Niue	.035
Tokelau	.003
Tonga	3.7
Tuvalu	.001
W. Samoa	7.2

SOURCE I

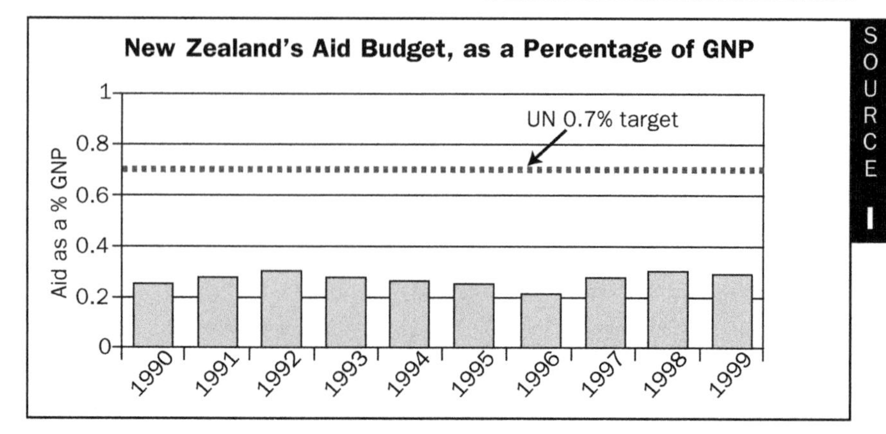

ACTIVITIES

Refer to Source F. Provide evidence to support your answers.

1 Which Pacific nation received the largest total amount of New Zealand aid from 1988 to 1992?

2 Which Pacific nation received the most aid per person?

3 Which Pacific nation received the smallest aid increase between 1988 and 1992?

Refer to Source G. Provide evidence to support your answers.

4 Which group of Pacific Islanders living in New Zealand remitted the most money home?

5 What might explain the difference between this group, and Niueans?

6 How *might* the level of remittances from Niueans living in New Zealand link to the level of aid given to Niue (Source F)?

Refer to Source H. Provide evidence to support your answers.

7 From which Pacific nation did New Zealand receive the greatest value of exports?

8 Look at the level of aid given to Niue (Source F) and the value of exports from Niue (Source H). One of the reasons stated for New Zealand's giving of aid is to try to build the economies of poorer nations. Is this likely to be the case with Niue? Explain your answer.

9 To which Pacific nation(s) is it most likely that New Zealand has given aid in the past, in order to develop the economy? Explain your answer.

Refer to Source I

10 What key idea(s) raised in this section of the text does this graph provide evidence for?

Aid from the Cook Islands Fundraising Committee to Prime Minister Lange in 1988 after Cyclone Bola devastated parts of New Zealand.

AS1.4 REVIEW ACTIVITY

In paragraphs of 100–150 words each, describe the perspectives (views) and actions (with an accompanying explanation) for the following:

1 New Zealand and greater involvement in the Pacific
2 National governments and the giving of aid
3 Prime Minister Norman Kirk and the giving of aid
4 Prime Minister Holyoake and Pacific Island migration
5 A Western Samoan migrant living in New Zealand in the 1970s
6 Pacific leaders and co-operation amongst Pacific nations
7 New Zealand governments and security issues in the Pacific.

AS1.5 ESSAY PRACTICE

Follow the steps outlined on the inside back cover to write the following essay.

For what reasons did New Zealand become involved in military actions in Asia between 1945 and 1970? What was New Zealand's relationship with Pacific Island countries after WWII?

- UN membership; ANZAM; ANZUS; SEATO
- South Pacific Commission; decolonisation; aid; immigration.

AS1.6 REVIEW ACTIVITY

1 Refer to the overview at the start of this section. Use the ideas there and the headings in the text to create a mind-map OR structured overview that shows the experiences that led to the shaping of New Zealand's identity with regard to the Pacific.

2 For both points below, write a 100–150 word paragraph.

- Describe actions taken by the New Zealand government after WWII to provide aid to the South East Asian region. (You may wish to review the section on SEATO, too.)
- Show how over time New Zealand developed a greater interest in the Pacific region.

CHAPTER SEVEN

NUCLEAR ISSUES

In terms of AS1.5 (essay writing – cause/course/consequences of an historical development) and AS1.6 (experiences that led to the shaping of a New Zealand identity) there were a number of key developments over nuclear issues.

OVERVIEW

After WWII, awareness of the destructive power of nuclear weapons led to a movement opposed to their construction, testing and use. New Zealand's anti-nuclear movement linked into this global organistion. From the late 1950s, the Labour Party began to adopt an anti-nuclear policy. However, the real boost to opposition came in 1966 when France relocated its nuclear testing programme from Africa to the Pacific. When Labour came to power in 1972 it took two very dramatic steps in an attempt to force French nuclear testing out of the Pacific. One was taking France to the World Court and the other was sending two Navy vessels to the testing zone. Ultimately these moves were both unsuccessful, but New Zealand had made a strong and independent stand. French actions were in the international spotlight.

Another dramatic development occurred in June 1985 when French agents bombed the Greenpeace protest vessel *Rainbow Warrior* in Auckland Harbour. To make matters worse, France actually threatened to block New Zealand's trade access to Europe if it did not release the jailed agents. New Zealand discovered again the limitations of being a small power. Despite this clear case of international terrorism and bullying, no major allies would support New Zealand's claim against France.

The nuclear issue took on another dimension as protest against the visits of (U.S.) nuclear powered or armed warships increased. At first, the focus was on environmental risks, but it later changed to moral opposition to nuclear weaponry. In another assertive action for a small nation, the Labour government – carried along by a huge wave of public feeling – banned the visit of nuclear warships. This angered the Americans, and in retaliation they declared ANZUS to be inoperative. Labour was also behind the creation of a South Pacific Nuclear-Free Zone. The extent to which being nuclear-free had become part of New Zealand's identity was made clear when National, which previously had not supported Labour's actions, also adopted the nuclear-free policy. When France resumed nuclear tests in the mid-1990s, National's Prime Minister Bolger sent a naval vessel to the test zone. He also reopened the earlier World Court case against France.

EXTENSION READING

Background to the nuclear issue

The testing and stockpiling of nuclear weapons by the major powers was an issue that increasingly concerned New Zealanders. As with the Vietnam War, the policies of Labour and National differed significantly. Nuclear issues were an important part of the wider Cold War. Supporters of nuclear testing and weapons argued that the weapons had a deterrent effect. It was, they said, only by keeping ahead of the Russians (and, later, the Chinese) that the West could feel secure. An enemy would know that if it attacked a Western country, a massive nuclear retaliation could follow. Opponents, however, pointed to the immorality of a few countries having the ability to decide whether or not to risk worldwide devastation. They also stated that nuclear weapons themselves were immoral because of the destruction and suffering they would cause to innocent civilians. The testing of nuclear weapons was criticised because it was seen as part of the process of becoming nuclear armed. It was also considered to be environmentally dangerous.

The development and testing of nuclear weapons began during WWII and continued in the Cold War era. By the 1970s, the United States, Britain, Russia, France, India and China were confirmed as having 'the bomb'. By the end of the 20th century, Israel and Pakistan were also believed to have secretly developed nuclear weapons. Nuclear testing in the Pacific region began in the 1950s. By the time the United States stopped testing there in 1962, it had exploded 106 bombs on Bikini Atoll and Enewetok. From 1952 to 1962 Britain exploded a total of 21 bombs – in the Australian outback, and on Montebello and Christmas Islands. By the time France stopped testing in the Pacific in early 1996, over 250 nuclear detonations had occurred.

Atom bomb.

EXTENSION ACTIVITIES

1 The Cold War ended in 1989, without the devastating nuclear war that opponents of nuclear weapons had warned of. Supporters of the deterrent effect of nuclear weapons claimed that they had been proved right. Do you agree with their view? Explain your answer.

2 France had been invaded and devastated in 1871, 1914 and 1940 (by Germany). It had been thrown out of its African and Asian colonies by the early 1960s. Was it justified in developing its nuclear capability in order to defend itself?

OPPOSITION TO NUCLEAR TESTING

New Zealand's official opposition to nuclear weapons and nuclear testing developed only slowly from the late 1950s. In 1957, the New Zealand government sent two naval vessels in support of British tests. This was despite calls since the end of WWII by many countries, including New Zealand, for a comprehensive ban on the testing of nuclear weapons. In 1950, over 20,000 New Zealanders signed a petition calling for 'the absolute banning of the atomic weapon'. Worldwide, 650 million signatures were gathered. This level of concern did not stop our government from putting in a bid to build a laboratory that could help process uranium for Britain's nuclear programme. Nor did it dampen talk of building a nuclear power station in New Zealand.

Nuclear testing in the Nevada desert, United States, 1952.

From the late 1950s nuclear issues became more prominent. During the campaign for the 1957 election, the Labour party began to express its own concerns about nuclear testing. Once elected, Labour was active in helping to bring before the United Nations a call for a Comprehensive Test Ban Treaty. Concern also grew from the early 1960s as New Zealand monitored the spread of radiation from U.S. testing in the Pacific. New Zealanders also tapped in to the growing international anti-nuclear movement. One of the largest groups was Britain's Campaign for Nuclear Disarmament (CND).

In 1959 a New Zealand branch of the CND was established. It held meetings and marches to raise public awareness. Over 80,000 New Zealanders signed its 1963 petition calling for a nuclear-free Southern Hemisphere – 'No Bombs South of the Line [Equator]'. Protest increased sharply when France shifted its nuclear testing programme from Northern Africa to the South Pacific.

United States nuclear testing at Bikini Atoll, in the Pacific.

ACTIVITY

Plot the key developments that led to growing opposition to nuclear testing on a timeline. Include only brief notes with an accompanying pictorial for each main point.

FRENCH NUCLEAR TESTING IN THE PACIFIC

When France carried out its first atmospheric test at Mururoa Atoll in 1966, it provided a focus for New Zealand's anti-nuclear campaign. Atmospheric testing – the exploding of a nuclear bomb above ground – allowed radiation and contaminated waste to be spread by the wind. This worst form of testing had been banned by international agreement in 1963, but it was now being carried out in the Pacific. What was more, France was not a traditional ally, even though New Zealand had fought on France's side in two world wars. Furthermore, France had not played a big role in the Pacific, despite its territories there. National's Prime Minister Keith Holyoake made a cautious protest to France, but he did not want to risk damaging trade opportunities with Europe.

By the 1970s, French atmospheric testing was attracting growing criticism. This came particularly from a new global movement, the environmental lobby. One of the organisations at the forefront of this movement was Greenpeace. In 1971, a poll showed that 82% of New Zealanders were opposed to French testing in the Pacific. When Labour came to power the following year, Prime Minister Norman Kirk pulled together these concerns in a direct challenge to French nuclear testing.

Although previous National governments had been opposed to nuclear weapons and testing, they were not active in condemning them: Labour under Norman Kirk was. In 1973 Kirk, in combination with the Australian Labor government, took France to the World Court over its nuclear testing. This was a bold and confrontational move; two small powers challenging a large power. The Court found against France and ordered it to stop its testing programme. France ignored the order. New Zealand discovered that its allies – particularly the United States and Britain – were unwilling to take any action to force France to comply. The ineffectiveness of the UN in enforcing its judgements was also exposed.

In the face of this lack of support from New Zealand's traditional allies, the nuclear movement began to take on a nationalistic flavour. A new petition against French nuclear testing gathered over 81,000 signatures. Individuals and private peace organisations – including Peace Media and Greenpeace – took matters into their own hands. Some sailed vessels into the test zone, although the French Navy dealt quickly and roughly with them. This caused anti-nuclear (and anti-French) sentiment to increase. Some of those who returned from the test zone in 1973 were awarded peace medals by the Mayor of Auckland. By 1976 60% of New Zealanders backed the anti-nuclear protest.

ACTIVITIES

Refer to Source A

1 What two countries are represented in this cartoon?

2 What is the 'joke' in this cartoon?

Refer to Source B

3 How did the situation shown in Source A lead to the action in Source B?

4 What, according to Prime Minister Kirk, was the role of the *Otago*? Use your own words.

SOURCE A

"Ah, mon ami – as always, we agree. You think I am about to explode the nuclear bomb in this vicinity. Voila! I think the same! France – New Zealand always in accord ..." (1964)

SOURCE B

'We are a small nation but we will not abjectly [helplessly] surrender to injustice. We have worked against the development of nuclear weapons. We have opposed their testing anywhere and everywhere .... Today the *Otago* leaves on an honourable mission. She leaves not in anger but as a silent, accusing witness with the power to bring alive the conscience of the world.'

Prime Minister Norman Kirk, farewelling the Navy ship Otago *in 1973. Kirk had notified 100 world leaders of his intention, seeking their support.*

The determination of the French to continue their atmospheric testing in the Pacific, and the lack of any real international pressure forcing them to stop, left New Zealand with a limited number of options. In another bold and even more confrontational move – rare for countries that are 'friendly' – Prime Minister Kirk ordered two Navy frigates to the Mururoa test zone in 1973. The Australian government provided a supply ship, without which the venture could not have taken place. Sending the frigates *Otago* and *Canterbury* was a stunning move. It shocked the French government and earned them instant unfavourable media attention.

In 1974 France moved its testing underground. This was seen as a victory of sorts for New Zealand, but the testing continued. The World Court felt that France had done enough and withdrew its ruling ordering them to stop. Many New Zealanders were dismayed by this decision, increasing support for Prime Minister Kirk's earlier action. The small South Pacific nation had taken a stand, even without the support of Britain or America.

National and Labour

New Zealand's position on nuclear issues depended very much on whether National or Labour was in power. When National became the government in 1975, with Robert Muldoon as Prime Minister, it did not pursue Labour's idea of a South Pacific nuclear-free zone. This was despite a poll showing that over 70% of New Zealanders supported the proposal. National was more concerned about not offending our traditional allies – and even France itself. The government at this time was desperately trying to maintain vital access to European markets for New Zealand's farm produce, against strong opposition from European farmers. National believed that New Zealand had to be realistic about its limited ability to influence major powers, and the potential cost to the country that its stance could cause.

THE *RAINBOW WARRIOR*

On July 10th 1985, French agents blew up and sunk the Greenpeace vessel *Rainbow Warrior* while it was anchored at the port of Auckland. The vessel had been preparing for another voyage to protest against French nuclear tests at Mururoa Atoll. Fernando Pereira, a Portuguese photographer on board at the time, was killed. Two of the ten or so French agents involved, Alain Marfart and Dominique Prieur, were soon captured by police. They were later sentenced in the Court to ten years' imprisonment although they did not actually do the bombing. At first, France denied any knowledge of the attack, but eventually it admitted responsibility. France then began to apply pressure to New Zealand to release its agents into French custody. Hints grew stronger that France would block New Zealand's trade into Europe if it did not comply. Prime Minister Lange accused France of 'a sordid act of State-backed international terrorism' but – as with the 1973 World Court ruling – New Zealand received little support from its allies. Only Australia condemned France. Britain and America refused to. The *Wall Street Journal* even supported the French action.

The Lange government felt obliged to accept the solution mediated by the Secretary General of the United Nations. Compensation of $13million was paid by France, and it promised not to interfere with New Zealand's access to European markets. New Zealand released the agents into French custody, for imprisonment on the French atoll of Hao. The public was angry that New Zealand had been bullied by France, and that there had been no international support over what was an act of terrorism. To make matters worse, the French government went back on its word. Within two years the agents were returned to France, complete with an official heroes' welcome. The whole incident thus became a defining moment in the development of an independent New Zealand identity.

AFTER THE *RAINBOW WARRIOR*

In 1992 France declared a short-term halt to nuclear testing. New Zealand hoped that this in fact marked the end of its programme. However, in 1995 testing resumed. National Party Prime Minister Jim Bolger immediately condemned the new blasts. France continued to deny that their testing posed any dangers to the environment, yet it refused to allow an independent scientific study. However, environmental concerns were only part of the issue. Along with other countries in the Pacific and beyond, New Zealand wanted France to sign a Comprehensive Test Ban Treaty. Countries that did so would agree not to test nuclear weapons at all.

Despite increasing pressure, France continued its tests. Prime Minister Bolger reacted angrily. 'France's insistence on continued testing has been outrageous. The overwhelming opposition to their testing programme can only be strengthened by the latest reports of radiation leakages at Mururoa as a result of earlier tests.' A New Zealand Navy vessel was sent to Mururoa and Bolger reopened the case against France in the International Court. Leaders at the 1995 Pacific Forum meeting also issued a challenge to French President Jacques Chirac. They called 'for an immediate end to all nuclear testing in all environments and for all states to work energetically for the early conclusion of an effective Comprehensive Test Ban Treaty ....' In early 1996 France detonated its sixth and last bomb in its series of tests. In March of that year France, Britain and the United States finally all signed the Comprehensive Test Ban Treaty. The issue of possible long-term damage at Mururoa had still not been settled by the year 2000.

ACTIVITIES

Refer to Source C

1. Provide evidence that supports the claim that the French were prepared for this sort of protest action.
2. How do you think the treatment of the protesters here by the French would have differed from the 'protesters' in Source B?
3. What is Alice Leney's view of the way that the French have treated her? Explain your answer.
4. How effective do you think this sort of protest action would be? Explain your answer.

SOURCE C

As well as government condemnation, private groups such as Greenpeace took action when France resumed its testing programme in 1995. On the tenth anniversary of the bombing of the original Rainbow Warrior, *the* Rainbow Warrior II *was seized by French commandos as it protested at Mururoa. The following report is from Alice Leney, who was part of a small team in an inflatable boat that evaded the French Navy and entered the restricted area of Mururoa Lagoon, in order to chain themselves to equipment used for nuclear testing.*

'We screamed up to this thing, and just as we came real close I realised you could drive a boat right in, right under the drilling rig itself.... Kate jumps up, I sort of slow the boat up, she grabs the walkway and I jump up.... At this point I see French Legionnaires running up the deck, so I quickly ... lock myself to the handrails on the drilling rig and sit down. Well, the French come screaming up ... three or four of them came and then they started wrenching at my arms because they thought I was just hanging on to the pipe .... [*The French soldiers cut through the chain lock.*] They carried me down, because we were non-violent protesters. They put us on a boat, they took us away to the gendarmerie [police] on the atoll.'

NUCLEAR SHIP VISITS

This issue of nuclear ship visits was tied in closely with opposition to French nuclear testing. Many of the same people who protested against France's actions also protested against having nuclear powered or armed vessels in New Zealand ports. The whole issue came to a head with the election of the Lange government in 1984. Earlier that year, the Muldoon government had called a snap election, hoping to increase its slim one-vote majority in parliament. The cause of the early election was the refusal of two National MPs, Marilyn Waring and Mike Minogue, to vote *against* Labour's proposed law to ban the visit of nuclear ships. National lost the election and Labour came to power, in part because of its anti-nuclear policy. The issue of nuclear ship visits had seen the fall of the National government; now it would sorely test the new Labour government.

Previously, government reaction to nuclear ship visits had changed from the 1960s on, and increasingly depended upon whether National or Labour was in power. Visits by British and U.S. vessels after WWII had been common. Between 1960 and 1984 there were nearly 150 visits by U.S. ships alone. Of these, only about 13 were nuclear-powered. In terms of weaponry, the United States had always had a policy to 'neither confirm nor deny' the presence of nuclear armaments on board its vessels. As nuclear concerns grew worldwide, both National and Labour wanted guarantees from the U.S. government. Mostly this was a requirement that compensation was to be paid if an accident occurred on a visiting nuclear-powered vessel. With no guarantee forthcoming, the National government banned U.S. nuclear-powered ships from 1969. In 1974, the U.S. agreed that it would pay compensation in the event of an accident. The following year, the new Muldoon government actively encouraged the visit of American warships, whether nuclear-powered or not. In the following eight years of Muldoon's government, an average of four US naval vessels visited each year. And each year, protest action grew.

Increasing Opposition

Muldoon's enthusiasm for visits by U.S. ships caused increasing public concern about the risk of a nuclear accident. In 1976, a 'Peace Squadron' was formed by members of St John's Theological College. It planned to block nuclear-powered vessels from entering Auckland's harbour. Public opinion polls showed a slow but steady increase in support for such actions. Between 1976 and 1982 opposition to the entry of nuclear-powered ships to New Zealand ports grew from 33% to 39%. Yet around 60% of people remained in favour of visits by American vessels, even if they were nuclear-armed. Most New Zealanders felt that it was in the country's best interest to maintain a strong alliance with the United States.

From 1979 the focus of the anti-nuclear movement began to shift as the possibility of a nuclear war suddenly became greater. One reason for this increased risk was the invasion of Afghanistan by the Soviet Union. No one was quite sure how the U.S. would respond to the Soviet aggression. The situation appeared to worsen considerably with the election of Ronald Reagan as American president in 1981. Reagan dramatically increased spending on the military and took a more confrontational stance with regard to the Soviet Union.

As the risk of a nuclear confrontation seemed to grow, nuclear war became more of an issue than environmental concerns about a nuclear accident. In 1981, the Auckland suburb of Devonport – the site of New Zealand's major naval base – took the symbolic action of declaring itself to be nuclear-free. Within two years another 37 local authorities had followed suit. In 1982, Christchurch became the first city to declare itself nuclear free. A year later, more than 35,000 people turned out to protest against the arrival of the USS *Truxton* in Auckland. Waterfront unions added their support to the anti-nuclear cause by going on strike. Some 400 different groups, covering a broad range of New Zealand society, were now represented in the anti-nuclear movement. By 1984, polls showed that 70% of people did not want ships capable of carrying nuclear weapons to come to New Zealand. That year, National lost the snap election and Labour swept into power, riding the wave of anti-nuclear feeling. David Lange, the new Labour Prime Minister, would now have to fulfil his party's election promise of making New Zealand nuclear-free.

Prime Minister Lange now found himself caught between a public distaste for nuclear-armed ship visits, and an equally strong desire for the continuation of ANZUS.

continues on page 60

ACTIVITIES

Refer to Source D

1. Who is the person on the right most likely to represent?
2. What is the 'joke' in this cartoon?
3. How might Prime Minister Muldoon (Source E) respond to the ideas shown here?

SOURCE D

Eric Heath, 1983

ACTIVITIES

Refer to Source E

1 Which country does Prime Minister Muldoon say 'has the power to realise the ideals we all share'?

2 What does Muldoon suggest could be the consequences of not being a 'reliable ally'?

3 What do you think would be Muldoon's response to the views expressed in Source B (page 54)?

SOURCE E

'New Zealand can do most to help maintain peace by continuing to act as a reliable ally of the United States... If we, as a community that tries to uphold Western values, have a contribution to make, we can make it most effectively by working with the one country that has the power to realise the ideals we all share.'

Prime Minister Muldoon, reaffirming in 1981 New Zealand's commitment to ANZUS, and supporting President Reagan's approach to dealing with the Soviet Union

Refer to Source F

4 What is the cartoonist's view of the British government's training course?

5 Look at Source D, also by the same cartoonist. Are these cartoons biased, or just realistic? Explain your answer.

SOURCE F

Eric Heath, 1983

Refer to Source G

1 In a quote of no more than five words, identify ONE opinion.

2 What caused the sights described in this source?

3 Describe the link between the description given here, and the key idea in Source F.

4 How might this experience have influenced David Lange in his role as Prime Minister?

5 How reliable is this as an historian's source? Explain your answer.

SOURCE G

'In the sky above Otahuhu the moon turned to blood ... As I walked from the bus stop to my home on a cold winter evening I saw an eerie lightening of the sky. Beams of light radiated from the northern horizon and intersected with each other through the blackness of the night ... the sky pulsated with these brilliant shafts of light. They were red and white. They extended across the night like the ribs of a fan. They were spinning, they were inter-mingling. The sky was diffused with a ghastly brush of red. It was an unnerving spectacle.'

David Lange recalls seeing the effects of an American atmospheric nuclear test above Johnston Island in the Pacific in 1962, the same year as the Cuban Missile Crisis.

Refer to Source H

6 How did the sort of event described in Source G lead to the situation in Source H?

SOURCE H

'One day when New Zealand and the United States were still on speaking terms he [Gerald Hensley, head of the External Intelligence Bureau] padded into my office to bring me sombre news. He had just been informed, he said, that the American early-warning system had picked up Soviet missiles heading for the continental United States. It looked, he continued, as if nuclear war had finally happened. In twenty minutes we'd know for certain. There wasn't anything I could do about it and, not wishing to start a panic among the staff, I sat signing letters while the minutes dragged past. Hensley came back. False alarm. It must have been a fault in the electronics, or a close formation of Canadian geese....'

Prime Minister Lange in 1984, during the period when President Reagan pursued an aggressive policy towards Russia.

Refer to Source I

7 What is the 'fuss' that the Captain is talking about?

8 What *particular* nuclear concern is this cartoon commenting on?

9 Explain the different concerns about the nuclear issue that the cartoons in Source I and Source F represent.

SOURCE I

Around 70% of New Zealanders wanted to ban nuclear ship visits, but the same proportion wanted to stay part of ANZUS, the defence treaty signed with America and Australia over 30 years earlier. Lange was very aware of this contradiction, and the apparent public belief that America would accept an ANZUS alliance without nuclear ship visits. Lange had very little room for manoeuvring. Earlier, he had tried to convince the Labour party membership to soften its position. The membership had reacted by voting for the complete withdrawal of New Zealand from ANZUS. Lange rejected this, because he knew it would be unpopular with New Zealand voters. On the other hand, he also knew that he could not compromise the party's anti-nuclear position without causing a damaging revolt in his own party. In 1983, the Labour Party membership again made their views very clear. Party President Jim Anderton stated: *'A nuclear-free Pacific must mean exactly that. No nuclear powered or nuclear armed warships must have New Zealand ports as a base, no matter what flag they fly.'*

Prime Minister David Lange

THE END OF ANZUS

Lange knew that the whole nuclear ship issue would come to a head when the United States next requested permission for a ship to visit New Zealand. He tried to convince U.S. officials to send only vessels that could not possibly carry nuclear weapons. The U.S. almost complied, by announcing in late 1984 that they would like to send the USS *Buchanan*. This ship was not nuclear-powered and nor was it of a type that usually carried nuclear weapons. It seems likely that the Americans believed that the *Buchanan* would be acceptable to the Lange government. The US Navy, however, would still 'neither confirm nor deny' whether there was any nuclear weaponry on board. This was not good enough to satisfy the Labour party membership. Nor did it satisfy the 10,000 protesters who turned out at a march to express their opposition. Lange could not be seen to be making any deals. In early 1985 he announced that permission for the *Buchanan* visit had been refused.

The Americans reacted angrily, although the importance to the United States of such a small South Pacific nation should not be overstated. (US Secretary of State Kissinger dismissed New Zealand as a 'dagger pointed at the heart of Antarctica.' Another critic called New Zealand 'a piss-ant little country south of nowheresville.') Nonetheless, America felt that it could not be seen to be backing down. Other countries, such as Norway, Denmark and Japan might follow New Zealand's example. According to the view of the US military, this could leave gaps in its nuclear capability with regard to the Soviet Union. Another reason for American anger was that some key U.S. officials had a personal dislike of Lange and his attitude. Furthermore, the United States did not like a small country like New Zealand

AS 1.1/1.2 ACTIVITY: SELECTING RELEVANT EVIDENCE

Provide evidence from the 'Nuclear Ship Visits' section (pages 56–57 and 60) to support each of the key ideas below. Evidence can include facts, statistics, quotes or similar.

1. Some members of Muldoon's National government actually supported Labour's anti-nuclear policy.
2. New Zealand had been regularly visited by allied warships, prior to the nuclear ban.
3. The American Navy did not want it publicly known whether its vessels were nuclear armed or not.
4. In the late 1960s, the National government was concerned about the cost of a nuclear accident.
5. Muldoon's National government encouraged visits by American warships, whether they were nuclear capable or not.
6. From the late 1970s, there was increasing public concern about the visits of nuclear ships.
7. Despite opposition to nuclear capable vessels, New Zealanders still wanted to remain part of ANZUS.
8. By the early 1980s, it seemed that the risk of nuclear war was growing.
9. From the 1980s, a broad cross-section of New Zealand society was opposed to nuclear capable ships.
10. By 1983, the Labour Party membership was totally opposed to any softening of Labour's anti-nuclear position.

attempting to dictate US policy. This was despite the fact that there had never been a requirement under the terms of the ANZUS Treaty to accept visits by the American military, whether nuclear or not. Lange felt that the Americans' unwillingness to compromise was unreasonable.

In terms of retaliatory actions taken by the US, all military and intelligence links with New Zealand were immediately cut. There were threats of other actions, including cutting off New Zealand's trade access to US markets, but these did not eventuate. This time, not even Australia would support New Zealand's position. Although Lange continued to negotiate with the United States into 1986, neither side would budge. The meltdown of the Soviet nuclear reactor at Chernobyl helped strengthen New Zealand's viewpoint, but had no influence on the Americans. ANZUS was officially declared to be 'inoperative' and New Zealand was downgraded from being an 'ally' to a 'friend'. Secretary of State George Schultz summed up the new situation: 'We part company as friends, but we part company.'

continues on page 63

ACTIVITIES

Refer to Source J

1 What has apparently been the effect of New Zealand 'shoving a potato up the exhaust pipe' of America's nuclear policy?

2 What, in reality, is the 'potato' referring to?

3 This cartoonist is using irony. What is the point that he is making about America's nuclear capability, and the *actual* effect of New Zealand's action?

SOURCE J

Bob Brockie, 1984

SOURCE K

Refer to Source K

4 What countries does each of the three figures represent? Provide evidence to support your answer.

5 In what way could this cartoon be said to show an anti-American bias?

6 What two conflicting views about nuclear issues are shown here? Provide evidence to support your answer.

7 What ONE idea about America's nuclear capability is expressed in this cartoon, as well as in Source D and Source J?

ACTIVITIES

Refer to Source L

1. The leaders of what two countries are represented here?
2. What does the cartoonist suggest will happen if the anti-nuclear speech *is* read at the United Nations?
3. Why would New Zealand be concerned about the 'thread' being cut? (Think about the sort of products New Zealand exports.)
4. On what other occasion did New Zealand come under similar pressure over nuclear issues? (Refer to page 55.)

Refer to Source M

5. According to the cartoon, what country is responsible for the break-up of ANZUS? Explain your answer. Is this view accurate?
6. Study the cartoon carefully. In terms of defence capability, what, according to the cartoonist, is ANZUS actually losing by NZ's 'withdrawal'?
7. What is the significance of Prime Minister Lange saying 'we will neither confirm nor deny'?

Refer to Source N

8. Give TWO pieces of evidence from the cartoon that show that New Zealand's departure from ANZUS was not a positive experience.
9. Compare the views here with those in Source M. In what ways are they similar, and in what ways are they different?
10. Identify a key idea in the text from this section that Lange's comment in Source N appears to support (see page 61).

Refer to Source O

11. In what period were exports to the United States highest (as a percentage of all exports)?
12. Provide evidence from the table that shows that New Zealand's trade with the United States did not suffer significantly because of its nuclear policy.

SOURCE L

Bob Brockie, 1984

SOURCE M

Eric Heath, 1985

SOURCE N

Sidney Lodge, 1986

SOURCE O

Exports from NZ to the US, as a percentage of total NZ exports, 1950–2000	
1950	10%
1960	13%
1970	16%
1980	14%
1990	13%
2000	14%

Although Labour's policy came under intense pressure from the U.S. and other countries, it was immensely popular in New Zealand. In June 1987 New Zealand's anti-nuclear legislation finally finished its journey through parliament and became law. Support for the nuclear ban remained high at around 70%. Support for remaining part of ANZUS – *if* the U.S. accepted New Zealand's anti-nuclear position – was as high as 80%. Proof of the extent to which the anti-nuclear position had become part of New Zealand's identity came in 1990. National Prime Minister Jim Bolger announced that his government would not change the anti-nuclear law. This was despite earlier claims by National that Labour was opening the way for the Soviet Union to enter the South Pacific.

The Labour government did all it could to maintain friendly relations with the U.S., and to repair relations with Australia. Some people called for the closure of U.S. installations such as the Antarctic Deep Freeze base at Christchurch and the observatory at Marlborough. The government refused, emphasising that New Zealand was 'anti-nuclear, not anti-American.' Although Australia disapproved of New Zealand's stance, links between the two countries actually strengthened. This was especially so when the Labour government agreed in 1989 to buy two expensive frigates from Australia, despite a poll showing that 76% of the public were opposed. The Lange government felt that New Zealand had to contribute its fair share to defence in the region, even if New Zealand was no longer an active member of ANZUS.

ACTIVITIES

Refer to Source P

1. What idea(s) in the first sentence are also reflected in Source L and Source O?
2. In your own words, what 'at worst' was Sir Geoffrey trying to do?
3. What is meant by the term 'blindly patriotic South Sea outpost'? Do you think that the editor of the *Christchurch Star* has made a fair analysis of New Zealand by the mid-1980s? Explain your answer.

SOURCE P

The following is an editorial from the Christchurch Star, responding to comments made by the British Foreign Secretary, Geoffrey Howe, that were critical of the Labour government's anti-nuclear legislation.

'At best Sir Geoffrey's remarks were thinly veiled threats that New Zealand could suffer in trade terms .... At worst, a remarkably unsophisticated attempt to sway New Zealand voters away from the Government.... This country is no longer the blindly patriotic South Sea outpost that it once was. There is now an independence and a sense of nationality that make his clumsy attempt at influencing New Zealand's affairs deeply offensive.'

McKinnon, p.299

Refer to Source Q

4. Why, according to the cartoon, is Prime Minister Lange being thrown out of the café? What does this mean in relation to the ANZUS situation?
5. What appears to be Lange's reaction to being thrown out? Explain your answer.
6. Identify a key idea from the text on this page that shows that Lange did not want New Zealand to be seen as a 'free-loader'.

SOURCE Q

ACTIVITY: THE END OF ANZUS

Some of the statements below contain errors. Correct them, and then provide evidence from the text in this section (pages 60, 61 and 63) to support the corrected statements.

1. The request by the Americans in 1980 to send the USS *Bucketon* on a visit to New Zealand was acceptable to many, because of the unlikelihood of it carrying nuclear weapons.
2. America believed that New Zealand's allowing of the USS *Buchanan* to visit could cause Russia to launch a nuclear attack.
3. Despite the severe actions taken against New Zealand by Britain, relations with America remained reasonably friendly.
4. By the late 1970s Labour's nuclear policy had become a feature of New Zealand's identity as a nation.
5. The Labour government was determined that its anti-nuclear policy should not be seen as anti-American.

A NUCLEAR-FREE SOUTH PACIFIC

Britain and the United States had conducted nuclear tests in the Pacific since the 1950s. New Zealand's position on this had been somewhat inconsistent. On the one hand, it had supported efforts to have the testing of weapons banned, while on the other it had been involved in British testing. It was French nuclear testing, beginning in 1966, which led to the first call for its banning in the South Pacific. Labour Prime Minister Norman Kirk was active in this campaign. He included a plan for a nuclear-free South Pacific at the same time as he took the French to the World Court and sent the Navy frigates to Mururoa (see page 55). However, it was not until the height of Lange's Labour government in 1985, and its anti-nuclear policies, that a South Pacific Nuclear Free Zone was established.

1979 – Auckland protest against a visit by nuclear attack submarine USS *Haddo*.

1976 – Protest against nuclear warships in Wellington harbour.

The Treaty of Rarotonga, as it was called, was signed on August 6th 1985, forty years to the day after the first atomic bomb was dropped on Hiroshima during WWII. Most of the members of the Pacific Forum signed. In doing so they agreed not to produce, store, test, dump or use nuclear materials in the South Pacific. The main limitation of the Treaty was that it could not outlaw the shipping of nuclear material through international waters. Nor did it prevent individual nations from allowing visits by nuclear vessels. The one significant thing that it did do was prevent the establishment of any further nuclear bases in the South Pacific. Thus, the main purpose of the South Pacific Nuclear Free Zone was to send a message to larger powers to respect the wishes of the nations of the South Pacific. By signing, both Australia and New Zealand showed their solidarity with their smaller neighbours. The Treaty was offered to France, Britain and the United States to sign, but all three refused. The Soviet Union did sign. The Pacific Forum thus found its proposal rejected by its allies and accepted by its one main potential 'enemy'.

ACTIVITY: A NUCLEAR-FREE SOUTH PACIFIC

Use the following key ideas to make your own brief notes about the Treaty of Rarotonga.

- Inconsistent early policy
- Plans for a nuclear-free Pacific
- The Treaty: pros and cons
- Signatories

SOURCE R

Refer to Source R

1 When and where was the first Nuclear Weapons Free Zone established?

2 What five nations are shown with nuclear capability? What characteristic(s) do they all have in common?

3 Look back to the 'Background' section (page 52). Quote the slogan of the anti-nuclear organisation *Campaign for Nuclear Disarmament* which had, by 1996, become a reality.

AS1.4 REVIEW ACTIVITY

In paragraphs of 100–150 words each, describe the perspectives (views) and actions (with an accompanying explanation) for the following issues:

1. French nuclear testing in the Pacific.
   - Labour Prime Minister Norman Kirk
   - Greenpeace, the Peace Squadron and/or other protest movements
   - National Prime Minister Jim Bolger
2. The bombing of the *Rainbow Warrior* and/or the arrest of the French agents
   - Labour Prime Minister David Lange
   - French Prime Ministers Laurent Fabius/Jacques Chirac
3. Visits by nuclear armed/powered vessels
   - Labour Prime Minister David Lange
   - Greenpeace, the Peace Squadron and/or other protest movements
   - New Zealand's traditional allies (Britain and America)
   - Prime Minister Robert Muldoon
4. South Pacific Nuclear Free Zone
   - Labour Prime Ministers Norman Kirk and David Lange

AS1.5 ESSAY PRACTICE

Follow the steps outlined on the inside back cover to write the following essay.

What nuclear issues faced New Zealand in the period 1973–1985? Describe New Zealand governments' reactions to these issues during this period.

- Nuclear testing; ship visits; ANZUS relationship
- International Court of Justice; protests; Muldoon; anti-nuclear laws

AS1.6 REVIEW ACTIVITY

1. Refer to the overview at the start of this section. Use the ideas there and the headings in the text to create a mind-map OR structured overview that shows the experiences that led to the shaping of New Zealand's identity with regard to the Pacific.
2. For each point below, write a 100–150 word paragraph.
   - **a** Describe actions taken by the Kirk Labour government (1972–75) that showed its opposition to French nuclear testing in the South Pacific.
   - **b** Show how after WWII New Zealand demonstrated an increasing concern for issues affecting the South Pacific.
   - **c** Describe actions taken by the Lange Labour government (1984–89) that showed its opposition to visits by nuclear capable vessels.
   - **d** Show how from 1960 differences developed between National and Labour over foreign policy issues.

NEW ZEALAND'S INTERNATIONAL RELATIONS BY THE END OF THE 20TH CENTURY

In the 55 years after the end of WWII, New Zealand's view of itself and its place in the world had changed dramatically. The links with Britain that were so important up to the early 1970s were almost entirely gone. Those that did remain were through the Commonwealth. In addition, many young New Zealanders continued to do their 'OE' to England. Britain, however, was no longer important in terms of trade or defence; even visits here by the Queen passed almost unnoticed. Britain, in turn, had few remaining commitments in this area of the world.

The United Nations, by contrast, was an even more important part of New Zealand's foreign policy at the end of the century. This was because the security situation had changed. South East Asia was no longer New Zealand's line of 'forward defence'. Communism there was no longer seen as a threat. Furthermore, by 1989 the 'Cold War' had ended. The need for defensive treaties such as ANZAM, SEATO and ANZUS had thus disappeared. In addition, relations with traditional allies such as Britain and America had also changed. New Zealand thus looked to a greater peacekeeping role, especially in the Pacific region. Australia was seen as an important partner in this policy.

The nuclear issue in the South Pacific – indeed, the Southern Hemisphere – was resolved to New Zealand's satisfaction. It did have a cost, in terms of a falling out with a significant ally, but the threatened trade reprisals did not eventuate. The nuclear issue, more than any other, gave New Zealanders a strong sense that their country was at last asserting its right to an independent foreign policy. As part of this policy, the Pacific had become more important. Immigration had made Auckland the largest Polynesian city in the world, and this was starting to be reflected in aspects of New Zealand's wider culture. One area, however, where New Zealand was still not meeting its international obligation was aid. New Zealand's continuing economic vulnerability was often given as the reason for this. Of the aid that it did give, the biggest part by far went to the Pacific.

Anzac Day – the growing numbers attending such services suggest that this day has become an important part of New Zealand's identity.

SELECT BIBLIOGRAPHY

Belich, J. *Paradise Reforged: A History of the New Zealanders from the 1880s to the Year 2000*, Penguin, Auckland, 2001
Brockie, B (ed), *I Was There: Dramatic First-Hand Accounts From New Zealand's History*, Penguin, Auckland, 1998
Brooking, T and P. Enright. *Milestones: Turning Points in New Zealand History*, Dunmore Press, Palmerston North, 1988
Hoadley, S. *The New Zealand Foreign Affairs Handbook*, OUP, Auckland, 1992
King, M. *The Penguin History of New Zealand*, Auckland, 2003
McKinnon, M. *Independence and Foreign Policy: New Zealand in the World Since 1935*, AUP, 1993
Ministry of Defence, *New Zealand Defence Quarterly*, Issues 21, 25, 27–29
Sinclair, K (ed). *The Oxford Illustrated History of New Zealand*, OUP, Auckland, 1996

PHOTOGRAPH ACKNOWLEDGEMENTS

The Alexander Turnbull Library, National Library of New Zealand, Te Puna Matauranga o Aotearoa for page 3 Display of frozen export carcasses outside the British New Zealand Meat Company, Christchurch 1/1-009113; Lloyd, Trevor 1863-1937: Kiwi; I think I would look better without it. Dominion. [1907?], C-109-023; page 4, Michael Joseph Savage on the campaign trail, 1/2-051739, F; US troops, Wellington, Freelance Collection; page 5, Prime Minister, Sidney Holland and Minister of Social Security, Eric Halstead, with Australian representative, sign Social Security Agreement with Australia, December 1955,1/2-177039, F; page 6, Headquarters of 16 NZ Field Regiment in Korea, with kiwi symbol,1/2-121222,F; page 9, Vote Communist; more community centres, more gas, more transit housing, improved parking facilities, more playing fields, better transport facilities. [ca 1944], Eph-D-ROTH-Communist-1944-02; Scott, Thomas: It says here, in the New York Times, that capitalism has finally triumphed over communism ... – this means our side won!! We did? [31 October 1989], H-196-023; page 12, Prime Minister Peter Fraser being greeted by Secretary of State, Cordell Hull, Washington DC,1/1-013281,F; page 15, Clark, Laurence, 1949-: I'm afraid the reports are not looking good. Arms Industry – Kampuchea; Afghanistan; The Gulf. New Zealand Herald, 16 August 1988, A-289-059; page 16, Crowd at Aotea Quay, Wellington, as K-Force troops leave on the Ormonde, K-0123, F; Australian and New Zealand personnel at Anzac Park, near forward defensive positions in Korea, K-0457, F; A gun of the 16th Field Regiment in action, Korea; PA1-q-312-1155; page 19, Clark, Laurence, 1949-: Hang on! Wait for me! New Zealand Herald, 4 December 1990, H-189-001; Evans, Malcolm 1947-: I'm concerned at the difference between what we and the Aussies get for being here!, New Zealand Herald, 2 August 2000, H-643-007; page 22, page 94, Sid Holland and Keith Holyoake, August 1957, 1/2-177291; page 23, F; Minhinnick, Gordon (Sir), 1902-1992: Better not interfere, old boy – he might lose his temper! Malaysia. 7 January 1964, E-549-q-13-004; page 25, Bromhead, Peter, 1933-: ANZUS Security Blanket. 9 November 1982. Everywhere I see Russians! Millions of them! Pouring into the Pacific! Armed to the teeth! I think I'm going to have to sell you a new security blanket to cope. 9 November 1982, A-305-165; page 34, Athletic Park 1921, Sydney Charles Smith, G-22973-1/1; All Black – Maori issue; sign the protest petition against racial discrimination. [1959], Eph-C-RACIAL-1959-01; page 35, Citizens All Black Tour Association: Protest meeting, Wellington Town Hall – Wednesday 12th Aug. at 8 p.m. No Maoris – No tour. [1959], Eph-D-RACIAL-1959-01; page 38, Scott, Thomas 1947-: Halt the tour! The tour must be stopped!! Or... aah... or... um... because... otherwise... aah... um... gosh... because... well... aah... um... gulp... people like me will become utterly irrelevant... 30 July 1992; H-110-022; New Zealand Public Service Association: Fight apartheid! Stop the tour. Their sport ... our politics. Mobilise – July 3rd. Assemble 6.30 pm Marion Street / published by Wellington Sections PSA [1981], Eph-C-RACIAL-1981-03; page 39, Ball, Murray: Okay, step forward any lyin' commy who says that the fact that I support the South African apartheid system and am also minister of police has anything to do with the present situation in this country. [1981]; A-323-060; page 43, Captain Anderson and his gun crew on horseback in Samoa during WWI,1/2-148856; F; New Zealand marines transporting Mau prisoners; PA1-o-795-12-1; Mau parade along Beach Road in Apia, Samoa, on Black Saturday, 1/2-019638; F; page 44, The Queen of Tonga inspecting her soldiers, Tonga, 1/2-082384, F; page 48, Scott, Thomas 1947:Welcome to 'Ethnic cleansing' 13 May 1993, H-046-009; page 49, Colombo Plan conference, Wellington, 1/2-177162, F; page 54, Minhinnick, Gordon (Sir), 1902-1992, 28 July 1964, E-549-q-13-005; page 58, Heath, Eric Walmsley, 1923-: You certain all this can prevent a nuclear war? DEAD CERTAIN! [9 May 1983], B-144-020; page 59, Heath, Eric Walmsley 1923-: Can't understand all this fuss they're making over radiation! [The USS Buchanan arrives in the harbour. 8 March 1985]; H-302-00x; page 61, Brockie, Bob, 1932-: U.S. Nuclear policy. Fizzz. Those asshole New Zealanders have shoved a potato up our exhaust pipe. [National Business Review, 1984]; Heath, Eric Walmsley 1923-:Big 3 Anzus meeting. "Is there some reason we can't all support a nuclear free zone, gentlemen?" [Dominion, 27 February 1974]; C-132-124; page 62, Brockie, Bob, 1932-:7 million tons U.S. surplus dairy produce. U.N. anti-nuclear speech. Feel free – say what you like. 1 October 1984, A-314-2-001; Heath, Eric:`Well, what about it, Mr Lange?'. The Dominion 28 August 1985, H-459-004; Lodge, Nevile Sidney, 1918-1989: N.Z. "I just never thought they'd really cast us adrift – It's as simple as that!" 12 December 1986, B-136-485; page 63, Scott, Tom,:Cafe ANZUS. Get outa here ya free-loader!! Todays special. Fission chips. I wasn't hungry anyway... 5 July 1986, A-312-4-001.

The Dominion Post Collection, Alexander Turnbull Library, Wellington for page 22, SAS during Malayan Emergency, M-0515; page 29, NZ Medical team in Bong Son, Vietnam; PAColl-7327; page 36, Robert David Muldoon, F-22486-1/4; Demonstrators outside South African consulate, Wellington, 1977; EP/1977/4807/8a; page 37, Protesters in Wellington during the 1981 Springbok tour; EP/1981/2884/11a; page 42, St Bernards College Polynesian Club; PAColl-7327; page 45, Colonel Rabuka, Fiji; EP/1987/2600; page 51, Cook islands Fundraising Committee presents a cheque to David Lange for Cyclone Bola relief fund; page 46, Kirikiti in Wellington; PAColl-7327; page 47, Jung Lee and family from Korea; EP/1979/1177/4a; page 60, Prime Minister David Lange hosting Radio Windy breakfast show, EP/1985/4912/9; page 110, Members of Campaign Against Nuclear Warships in Wellington Harbour, EP/1976/2841/26a.

United States National Archives and Records Administration for the photographs on pages 4 (Pearl Harbour), 8, 12, 15 (Korean War), 26, 52, 53, 55, 66.

The Hocken Library, University of Otago, Dunedin for the posters on page 39, 'Is this the life for you?' (8998855); 'Mobilise to stop the tour' (8909928).

New Zealand Defence Force for the photographs on pages 18, 19, 20.

GLOSSARY

Apartheid See page 33

Boycott To refuse to trade, play sport or associate with someone, or a country. It is a means of applying pressure.

Bridge-building Prime Minister Muldoon's policy of continuing links with a country to try to encourage it to change their policies (see page 37).

Capitalism See page 8

Cold War See page 8

Collective security Where countries band together to support each other. An attack on one is regarded as an attack on all members (see page 4).

Colony A country that is governed by another, more powerful country, as part of an empire (see also 'Decolonisation'), which often also sends migrants.

Colonialism The practice by a more powerful country, of sending some of its population to settle in another country, and the governing of that country.

Communism See page 8

Conscription The compulsory call-up of men to join the Army.

Containment The United States believed that to stop the spread of communism they needed to boost military forces in neighbouring non-communist countries, thus 'boxing in' or containing communism (see also 'Domino Theory').

Decolonisation See page 44 (see also 'Colony').

Domino Theory The United States believed that if South Vietnam fell to communist forces, neighbouring countries would be next. They compared this to a row of dominoes being knocked over.

Foreign policy See page 3

Forward defence A military strategy of placing troops in a forward position to deter enemy attacks, rather than waiting in a rearward defensive position.

Guerilla warfare Military tactics often used by weaker forces against better equipped and more powerful forces, often involving ambushes and 'hit and run' attacks.

Left-wing See page 8

Mau A Samoan resistance group that was opposed to New Zealand's style of rule after WWI.

Military coup An illegal seizure of power by the Army or other Armed Forces.

Militia A miltary force that is made up of ordinary citizens rather than professional soldiers.

Veto The right of any one member of a group or organisation to oppose a planned action, thus stopping the action.